BASIC TRAINING

BASIC TRAINING

THE BATTLE BELONGS TO THE LORD

SV DOHERTY

Tate Publishing *& Enterprises*

Published by Tate Publishing & Enterprises, LLC
127 E. Trade Center Terrace | Mustang, Oklahoma 73064 USA
1.888.361.9473 | www.tatepublishing.com

Tate Publishing is committed to excellence in the publishing industry. The company reflects the philosophy established by the founders, based on Psalm 68:11,
"The Lord gave the word and great was the company of those who published it."

Book design copyright © 2008 by Tate Publishing, LLC. All rights reserved.
Cover design by Leah LeFlore and Kaitlin Doherty
Interior design by Stephanie Woloszyn

Published in the United States of America

ISBN: 978-1-60604-845-0
1. Christian Living: Spiritual Growth: Spiritual Formation/Spiritual Warfare
2. Christian Living: Spiritual Growth: Prayer/Healing
08.09.02

ACKNOWLEDGMENT

My heartfelt thanks goes to my precious family, who encouraged and supported my endeavor to be obedient to the call of the Lord.

TABLE OF CONTENTS

FOREWORD

"For a long time Israel was without the true God, without a priest to teach and without the law." 2 Chronicles 15:3

Susan Doherty has captured for us the challenge of a basic boot camp approach to the Christian faith, while embracing apostolic Christianity for believers in all stages of their Christian walk. The challenge is that this book is a wonderful course in the basics of the faith, which are life-saving and a true preparation for the spiritual battles of life.

It not only contains the essentials of the faith—which are a must for the spiritually ready Christian soldier—but it is a teaching syllabus, applying personal spiritual principles from our field manual, the Bible.

To read, mark, and inwardly digest the next 100 pages or so is to become better equipped, spiritually challenged, and prepared to live a triumphant Christian life. This course is uniquely engaging, it is astonishingly proactive in encouraging the student, and it elicits the maturity in each of us, which can be translated into our individual ministries.

When Israel was without teaching priests and the word of God, she wandered. When the church is without willing and equipped teachers and soldiers, she too is ill prepared to answer the high call of her commander-in-chief, Jesus. Now, either sequentially page by page, picking the chapter of interest, or part by part, enjoy and become better equipped by this special book from the heart of a committed teacher and trainer of successful Christians.

Fr. Charles B. Fulton, Jr.
President
Episcopal Renewal Ministries

INTRODUCTION

In the dark stillness of the pre-dawn morning, I clicked on the lamp next to my chair. I sipped a steaming cup of coffee and snuggled a little farther under the little lambskin rug I'd grabbed to get warm.

I whispered tenderly into the quiet room, "Lord, I love you," and began my morning ritual of worshiping the Lord. As I sang my little made-up songs of praise and worship, I began to relax as I felt the calming peace of His presence slowly envelop the room.

Suddenly, as if someone had inserted a video clip into my mind, my peaceful thoughts were interrupted with a startling and disturbing picture. The moving picture revealed a dark, smoke-filled battle scene. Many people with vacant stares were wandering around aimlessly. Gunfire was ricocheting through the crowd, and bombs of all sizes were exploding unexpectedly in the midst of the people.

I puzzled over this distressing picture and wondered why the people weren't trying to avoid being hit by the mortars. Slowly, I began to perceive that the people were blind. They were walking directly into the line of fire because they couldn't see. In this tragic picture, the blind people were taking hit after hit from missiles and gunfire, and were wounded and dying.

As I mused over this unexpected and pitiful picture, my thoughts were again interrupted. I heard a startling commandment in my spirit, "*Write My book of faith.*"

My eyes flew open wide, and I said out loud, "Who, me? I'm not qualified to write a book about faith!"

Again in my spirit I heard, "*Write My book—My book of faith. Begin with the prophet Isaiah and go forward through Jesus. See what they did and how they did it.*"

In that instant I understood what the battle scene meant. The people were God's children. They were getting killed and wounded by their enemy because they couldn't "see" the enemy's tactics. Therefore they were defenseless against the onslaught.

It began to dawn on me that my heavenly Father wanted a book written to help His children understand spiritual things. He wanted them armed instead of defenseless when facing their battles in life.

With my eyes as large as my coffee cup, I argued with the Lord. I told Him emphatically that I wasn't qualified and couldn't write His book of faith. After all, there were already a lot of books written about faith by famous preachers. I firmly put the thought out of my mind.

For the next six months I couldn't escape the Lord's commandment echoing over and over again in my soul. I continued to tell the Lord I couldn't write His "book of faith," but several times a week the same disturbing picture would come back. Finally, like a tired fish on a line, I gave up the argument. I decided that if it were really Him that told me to do this work, He would enable me to do it.

I believe what He has placed in these pages through me is a simplified overview of the basics of true Christianity. His basics. Not doctrine or theology or a scholarly view of the scripture. But how to maintain a peace and calm in the midst of raging battles. How to overcome when there seems to be no way. And most importantly, how to really enjoy our Lord's magnificent presence.

CHAPTER 1

BATTLE READY

Part I—The Basics

Your Story

Have you ever had a day that was so bad you couldn't wait for it to be over? Of course, we all have. Stuff happens.

The Lord sees the burdens you carry. He knows when you feel unloved and unappreciated. It grieves Him when you struggle with physical and emotional difficulties.

The Creator of the universe wants to help you! He wants to become your burden bearer. To help, strengthen, and empower you to overcome troubles instead of them overcoming you. To equip you with the supplies and ammunition you need to overcome the battles you encounter in life.

The way we become equipped is through knowledge and use of His word in our lives, and an intimate relationship with Him.

It's time to lay all the worries down. To let God carry you. Deliver you. And help with what comes your way.

In the pages ahead, we'll explore how to appropriate and rest in the Lord's victory. We'll trust in the Lord for what we need in every circumstance. We will join the winning side as we develop a close relationship with our Leader and apply the truth that is in His word to our lives.

There Is a War Going On

The six months following my decision to make Jesus Lord of my life were spent blissfully unaware of our enemy.

During that time, I spent hours listening to tapes on faith, until my faith was to the level that every thing I prayed for was answered. Big and small, they were all answered!

Then I began to wonder why other people's prayers weren't always answered. I condescendingly concluded they just didn't know what they were doing. Then came a period of time when none of my prayers were answered. Not any!

That certainly got my attention. I wasn't doing anything different than when my prayers were being answered. Bewildered, I prayed frequently, "Why aren't my prayers getting answers now?"

The Lord began to teach me that sometimes our prayers are *blocked*. Answers to our prayers may be blocked by disobedience or wrong attitude on our part, or by something that I had up to this point been unaware of—the enemy.

In a quiet time with the Lord, I heard words in my spirit that shook me out of a self-made cocoon: *"Gird yourself up tightly. Ask for the supplies and ammunition that you need for today. Fill the holes in your walls with holy mortar, and I will surround you with My protection."*

I was shocked! I knew I didn't use words like "gird" and certainly didn't think in warfare terms. These words seemed incredibly to have been a message from God. It slowly began to dawn on me that if He was telling me I needed ammunition and protective walls, there must be a war going on that I was oblivious to. Logically, if there was a war, there must be an enemy to contend with.

Up to this point, I mistakenly thought that all Christians needed to do to walk in victory was to love the Lord and have faith in His promises. The Lord began to reveal that although these things are necessary, there is much more to be aware of in the spiritual realm.

In addition to peace, joy, and love, we need to add *discipline, training,* and *being prepared for enemy attacks* as survival skills in the spiritual arena.

Our heavenly Father wants us prepared because there is a prowling devil out there just waiting for the opportunity to eat us up (1 Peter 5:8).

I discovered in the following months that all preparation has to originate out of our relationship with our heavenly Father, our Lord Jesus, and our precious Holy Spirit. From that relationship comes an amazing protection that occurs as we let Jesus live in us and through us. When He lives and dwells in us, His protection radiates out of us and enables us to walk in His love and power.

> I have been crucified with Christ; and *it is no longer I who live, but Christ lives in me;* and the life which I now live in the flesh I live by faith in the Son of God, who loved me, and delivered Himself up for me. Galatians 2:20

We Have an Enemy

Most people I've come into contact with haven't learned much about the invisible spiritual world around us. So, just in case you haven't heard the Star Wars-like saga encased in the pages of scripture, we'll begin with the plot and "who's who" of our supernatural story...

Once upon a time, a beautiful, talented musician was part of the kingdom of heaven. He was so talented that he became the leader of God's choir of angels. Like a lot of us, he had too much pride for his own good, and he decided that he should be ruler of heaven. So he and his supernatural buddies went to war with God. By the way, the name of our character is Lucifer, otherwise known as Satan.

As you can imagine, that didn't go over very well with God, so Lucifer and his followers were banished from heaven. They came to earth and became rulers of what we know as the world.

After awhile, Jesus came to earth to make a way for the sinful people of earth to be reunited with their Creator. He came to show the love of our heavenly Father, and to fulfill the spiritual principles and practices necessary for that reconciliation.

Jesus gave His sinless earthly body as the perfect sacrifice for mankind's sins. This sacrifice substituted His goodness for our badness before God. When Jesus gave His life on the cross, His body died but His spirit didn't die. In the supernatural world, He went to Satan's throne and fought him for his crown. Jesus won, took Satan's crown, and made a show of Satan openly.

Jesus conquered Satan and his crew (Heb. 2:8), but He didn't kill them. Unfortunately, Satan was still allowed to rule what the Bible refers to as "the world," but his authority on earth became subject to Christ's authority. In simpler words, Satan still had power, but Jesus' power was stronger.

Fortunately, when we chose Jesus as our Lord, we came out from under the authority of Satan's kingdom called "the world," and came under the authority of Jesus' kingdom, called "heaven." This means we are now citizens of heaven. The only problem is we are living smack dab in the middle of Satan's kingdom, and he doesn't appreciate our not pledging allegiance to him.

We acquired a formidable, invisible enemy when we decided to make Jesus Lord of our lives. For *His enemies became our enemies* (Rev. 12:17) and *His allies became our allies* (Heb. 1:14).

If you are like I am, you may be thinking, *This is more than I bargained for! I don't want to fight anything or anyone.*

Thank God we don't have to! Jesus has already won

the victory. He took Satan's crown and authority. And then wonder of wonders, Jesus turned right around and gave that authority to us as his disciples. He even said we would do greater works than what He had done (John 14:12). But it is important to understand who or what we are up against if we are going to experience the victory Jesus died to give us.

Understanding Who the Enemy Force Is

If there are enemy forces trying to sabotage us, we need to know more about our opposition. Who are they?

> [Jesus said,] "Go into all the world and preach the gospel to all creation. He who has believed and has been baptized shall be saved; but he who has disbelieved shall be condemned. And these signs will accompany those who have believed: in My name they will cast out *demons,* they will speak with new tongues; they will pick up serpents, and if they drink any deadly poison, it shall not hurt them; they will lay hands on the sick, and they will recover." Mark 16:15–18

Jesus referred to demons in this passage as real entities. The word "demon" means evil spirit. Many of us in our upbringing were raised to believe that evil spirits belong in horror stories. But if we believe what Jesus said is true, we must acknowledge everything He said as truth, not just the things we can understand and would like to accept.

Jesus went out preaching, teaching, healing, and casting out demons His entire ministry. Aren't we supposed to do what He did? A scary thought, isn't it? That's because most of us haven't been taught about these things.

Unfortunately, demons are not all we have to contend with. There are various enemy forces we need to be aware of. Ephesians 6:12 says, "For our struggle is not against flesh and blood, but against *the rulers,* against *the powers,* against *the world forces of this darkness,* against *the spiritual forces of wickedness* in the heavenly places."

If that didn't convince you, here are some more verses that refer to supernatural powers and kingdoms:

When He had disarmed the *rulers* [*principalities*—KJV] and *authorities* [*powers*—KJV], He made a public display of them, having triumphed over them through Him. Colossians 2:15

For I am convinced that neither death, nor life, nor angels, nor *principalities,* nor things present, nor things to come, nor *powers,* nor height, nor depth, nor any other created thing, shall be able to separate us from the love of God, which is in Christ Jesus our LORD. Romans 8:38–39

[Jesus said,] "Now judgment is upon this world; now the *ruler* [*prince*—KJV] of this world shall be cast out." John 12:31

[Speaking of Jesus] For He delivered us from the *domain* [*power*—KJV] of darkness, and transferred us to the *kingdom* of his beloved Son. Colossians 1:13

Earthly principalities are small states or countries ruled by a prince and/or a supreme power. Spiritual principalities are *supreme powers that rule over a specific area.* They are not the highest or the lowest in our enemy's ranks.

We can get a little further insight into the spirit realm looking at a war story recorded in the book of Daniel. In response to Daniel's fasting and seeking Him, the Lord sent His angel in person to answer Daniel's questions.

Daniel describes his experience in awe:

> I lifted my eyes and looked, and behold, there was a certain man dressed in linen, whose waist was girded with a belt of pure gold of Uphaz. His body also was like beryl, his face had the appearance of lightning, his eyes were like flaming torches, his arms and feet like the gleam of polished bronze, and the sound of his words like the sound of a tumult.
>
> Then he said to me, "Do not be afraid, Daniel, for from the first day that you set your heart on understanding this and on humbling yourself before your God, your words were heard, and I have come in response to your words." Daniel 10:5–6,12

This passage describes a supernatural being—a warrior and a messenger for God—called an angel.

The angel told Daniel that he had been detained from coming to speak with him because of a confrontation with an enemy force. He was finally able to get away because Michael, who was Daniel's angel, came to help him. Michael had the title of "prince," which would refer to authority over a territory. He also told Daniel of spiritual forces with titles of "kings and princes" that he was fighting.

> [The angel said,] "But the *prince of the kingdom of Persia* was withstanding me for twenty-one days; then behold, *Michael, one of the chief princes,* came to help me, for I had been left there with the *kings of Persia.*"
>
> Then he said, "Do you understand why I came to you? But I shall now return to fight against the *prince of Persia;* so I am going forth, and behold, the *prince of Greece* is about to come. However, I will tell you what is inscribed in the writing of truth. Yet there is no one who stands firmly with me against these *forces* except *Michael your prince.*"
> Daniel 10:13, 20–21

In this dramatic scene, we get an inside picture of the *unseen* kingdoms that are operating while our *seen* kingdoms are taking place. We are told here about fallen angels who have taken over certain areas as their territory. Opposing them are the Lord's angels who make war against them.

A closer look shows us that:

1) Both sides have *titles*, which relate to *authority over kingdoms.* If there were no kingdoms, there would be no need for rulers.

2) Kingdoms consist of *subjects* or those under the

authority of a higher power, so obviously there are *lesser powers or beings within the principalities.*

3) There is a hierarchy in an *unseen world* operating around us that we are, for the most part, oblivious to.

This Means War

Satan has declared war on the followers of our Lord Jesus Christ. We are in a war zone. If you don't believe it, read this.

> *And the dragon was enraged with the woman* [figuratively Israel], *and went off to make war with the rest of her offspring, who keep the commandments of God and hold to the testimony of Jesus.* Revelation 12:17

Satan intends to make war with the followers of Jesus, and he doesn't play fair. He would like to kill us, and to steal our health, money, sound mind, or anything else he can get hold of. Ultimately he wants to destroy the "offspring" who keep the commandments of God and have the testimony of Jesus Christ.

Don't worry! Jesus stripped Satan and his crew of their authority (Col. 2:15) and took the keys of death and hell (Rev. 1:18). *As Jesus lives in us, we receive the benefit of His victorious triumph.*

We've all heard the war stories about lost soldiers who were found still fighting the enemy when the war was already over. Sometimes we try to fight the enemy when

Jesus has already won the war for us. Remember, our side won! *We are the victors* through Christ Jesus.

He has given us the victory, but how do we take it and apply it to our lives? Second Corinthians 2:14 says, "But thanks be to God, *who always leads us in His triumph in Christ,* and *manifests through us the sweet aroma of the knowledge of Him* in every place."

This tells us to take the *knowledge of Christ,* which is His word, and use it against the enemy when he attacks. That is what Jesus did when Satan came to tempt Him in the wilderness. Jesus said, "*It is written…*" (Luke 4:4, 8).

We can't let the enemy fool us into thinking we need to fight them. They are already defeated! We resist them by our strength in the Lord and *stand firm on Jesus—the Word, by using His word.*

Don't let Satan's kingdom steal your blessings. Resist them with the word. They have to flee, for it is written!

Be Filled and Resist

The enemy and his troops like to have a body to live in. They are always looking for an open door so they can have a territory to work on usurping.

You say, "What?! Are you talking demon possession here?" My answer is, not usually. But they can live in your flesh without possessing your spirit. They can also oppress you without being in you at all. But *when they have resided in you and are evicted, they will always try to come back.* Jesus gave us a frightening insight into what happens if we don't allow the Holy Spirit to fill us after we have been cleansed or delivered.

> [Jesus said,] *"Now when the unclean spirit goes out of a man, it passes through waterless places, seeking rest, and does not find it. Then it says, 'I will return to my house from which I came;' and when it comes, it finds it unoccupied, swept, and put in order. Then it goes, and takes along with it seven other spirits more wicked than itself, and they go in and live there;* and the last state of that man becomes worse than the first. That is the way it will also be with this evil generation." Matthew 12:43–45

We always have some spiritual housecleaning to do when we meet Jesus. We need to continue to "keep our house clean" all the days we are on earth. When we're filled with the Holy Spirit and eating, sleeping, and breathing the word in our lives, we won't have an "unoccupied house" for the enemy to inhabit.

Recognizing the effects of the enemy is important for our defense. Some effects we may see are guilt, condemnation, sickness, fear, poverty, mental illness, physical infirmities, lies, and all kinds of perverse and evil things.

If we don't resist them they can destroy us. But if we resist them firm in our faith, our God will deliver us! Remember, it is not our power that overcomes the enemy, but *the power of the Lord as He lives in us.*

> But *resist him [the devil] firm in your faith,*

knowing that the same experiences of suffering are being accomplished by your brethren who are in the world. And *after you have suffered for a little while, the God of all grace, who called you to His eternal glory in Christ, will Himself perfect, confirm, strengthen and establish you.* 1 Peter 5:9–10

Make no mistake, resisting is active, not passive! To resist is *to act against* or *to oppose.* It is not lying down and letting the enemy walk all over us while we wait patiently for our Father to come to the rescue! Sometimes there is a bit of a wrestling match to see who is stronger—the enemy or *our faith in God's deliverance.*

How do we resist? We turn our mind to what the word says concerning our circumstances. We remind ourselves that Jesus is the victor over Satan and anything less than victory in our circumstances is not allowable. Then we put our foot down and remind the devil *what the word of God says* about his defeat. It takes the word to properly resist an attack.

If I start to get a cold—stopping up…nose running… sneezing—I speak to the cold. I speak to it immediately, before it gets a chance to overcome me. I heard a preacher say one time it is a lot easier to get a snake off the front porch, than to wait until it gets in your house under the couch and has babies!

I call it by name, "Cold, I call you gone in Jesus' name. Sickness and disease, I do not allow you in my body. Go, in the name of Jesus. The word of God says Jesus bore my infirmities and took my diseases and by His stripes

BATTLE READY

I am healed. So I say I am healed and well by the power of Jesus and the blood of Jesus and the name of Jesus. Thank you, Jesus, for my healing!"

Then I start praising the Lord for His wonderful gift of healing that He died to give me. I praise Him until I get happy and joyful and forget about the cold symptoms. Later I'll notice that all the symptoms went away. God is so good! He is faithful, as we trust in Him.

We must say what we mean and mean what we say. *The word of God in our mouth and on our lips is the most powerful weapon in the arsenal! Resist* with it—Jesus did! Then the devil and his crew will have to flee!

"Submit therefore to God. *Resist the devil and he will flee from you*" (James 4:7).

You Are in the Army Now!

A Sunday school teacher I had in the fifth grade gave a great illustration that I've never forgotten. He held up a lone matchstick and said, "This is what you're like when you try to stand alone without other Christians," and quickly snapped it in two.

Then he took a large handful of matchsticks and put a rubber band around them and tried to break the bundle. They didn't break. He explained, "When they are banded together in a tight group, they are too hard to break. The united group has more strength."

We are like an army if we band together for protection, assistance, and comradeship. Our "army" is unique. We don't war with conventional weaponry. Our weapons are

32

spiritual. We stand on the principles outlined in the word of God, resist the enemy, and have faith our Leader will lead us through our battles to victory.

We each have an important part to play in our Lord's army. You may be called to be a private or a captain. Your area of service may be in supply or leader of the pack. Whatever it is, *there is a need for you to take your position.* Your life on earth and the lives of others depend on it.

Our Protection—The Holy Armor of God

Have I scared you? There is no need to worry, for Jesus knew we would need protective armor and the right weapons to protect ourselves from enemy attack. Because of that, He prepared the special armor we need. It is amazingly Himself!

> The night is almost gone, and the day is at hand. Let us therefore lay aside the deeds of darkness and let us *put on the armor of light.*
>
> But *put on the LORD Jesus Christ,* and make no provision for the flesh, in regard to its lusts. Romans 13:12, 14

The armor of light is Jesus. This scripture tells us to put on the armor of light or actually to "put on" Jesus.

How in the world can we do this? In Ephesians 6:11–17, we are given an armor "check list." Let's look at each protective piece and then we'll discover how to put on our "Jesus armor." You may want to open your Bible to Ephesians 6 and read this section as we learn how to dress ourselves for protection.

1) First, we *gird or surround our loins with truth* (Ephesians 6:14a). What exactly are loins? They are the part of our body that encompasses the abdomen and pelvis, including both sides of the lower backbone. This area represents the beginning point of physical strength and reproductive power.

Jesus told us our belly is where the Holy Spirit flows from. This is a tender, vital area that needs special protection. Jesus can become that protection, for He is the truth.

Jesus said, "I am the way, and the truth, and the life; no one comes to the Father, but through Me" (John 14:6). Ephesians 6:14 tells us to surround our loins with truth. As we surround ourselves with Jesus the truth, He becomes our armor.

Do you think Jesus can become our armor of truth if we are lying about things and deceiving people? I doubt it.

I have been trying my hardest to be honest with people since I made Jesus Lord of my life. Sometimes it's the most painful thing in the world to do! When the truth will get us into trouble with someone, our instinct is to "stay safe" and bend the truth or avoid it altogether. My family can repeat to you with relish the two times I got caught lying about something. And it wasn't even important! I don't even know why I did it. But I did and it has become memorable in a very unfavorable way. I can see now how stupid it was, and I'm sure provided an open door for the enemy.

Let's remember to not interfere with our Jesus armor, and speak the truth. Then as we allow Jesus to surround us with His truth, we'll have the protection our tender, vital areas need.

2) Next, we receive the *breastplate of righteousness* (Eph. 6:14b). The breastplate covers our upper body, which includes our "heart" or center of being. Since our spirit lives and dwells in our "heart" or center, this breastplate also protects our spirit.

Our breastplate is made out of righteousness. Jesus is the only one who can make us right or righteous, so He is our breastplate of righteousness.

> My little children, I am writing these things to you that you may not sin. And if anyone sins, we have an Advocate with the Father, *Jesus Christ the righteous;* and He Himself is the propitiation [satisfaction] for our sins; and not for ours only, but also for those of the whole world. 1 John 2:1–2

Jesus becomes our breastplate as He purifies us, making us right and sinless before the Father. According to the scripture, He does this *by the cleansing action of His supernatural, living blood.* Let me explain how this works…

Leviticus 17:11 says, "For *the life of the flesh is in the blood,* and I have given it to you on the altar to make atonement for your souls; for it is the blood by reason of the life that makes atonement."

The spiritual principle is righteous blood makes atonement or compensation for unrighteous souls. Jesus' blood was and is the only righteous blood, since He never sinned. His death and the giving of His life was the final sacrifice given to make atonement for unrighteous people. That's us.

Because Jesus is alive in a supernatural form, His supernatural blood has life. So when we place the supernatural, righteous blood of Jesus over our "heart," the righteous blood atones or cleanses us from what's not right.

The enemy has been and always will be defeated by the blood of Jesus (Rev. 12:11). They fear the blood of Jesus! They can't get through it. This is why it becomes our breastplate of protection.

I've had the opportunity to hear several people speak about their experiences as former Satan worshipers. They were very emphatic that the blood of Jesus makes evil spirits not able to operate. They said when Christians "use" or call forth the blood of Jesus as protection, the Satanist's power is ineffective in that circumstance.

I've also heard people give their testimonies about being delivered from evil spirits. They said that when the people who were praying for them invoked the blood of Jesus, the evil spirits in them went wild. They can't stand the blood of Jesus! It ultimately defeats them.

Keep your "heart," the dwelling place of your spirit, always shielded with the life and righteousness of Jesus—*His blood.*

3) Even our feet get special treatment! Jesus washed the disciples' feet to symbolize His cleansing them from the world's dirt. He spiritually washes our feet and puts on our *shoes of peace,* as we prepare others to receive the good news of His peace (Ephesians 6:15).

Jesus said, "Peace I leave with you; My peace I give to you; not as the world gives, do I give to you. Let not your heart be troubled, nor let it be fearful" (John 14:27).

We get His peace when we receive His presence into our lives. He brings His spiritual peace with Him—because He is peace!

He gave us the job of preparing the way for others to receive His presence (Acts 1:8). When we do, Jesus becomes all the protection we need against every obstacle that may come up in our path.

4) Next, we take up the very important *shield of faith* to protect us from *all* the flaming missiles of the evil one (Ephesians 6:16). "All" is a pretty big word. If we have our shield of faith in front of our armor, the missiles can't get to us! No matter what the enemy hurls at us, we stop it with our faith.

But what is faith? Faith, put simply, is the act of trusting and believing in our Lord and Savior and His promises.

God responds to our trust in Him and His promises.

I'm going to say that one again! God *responds* or reacts to our trust in Him and His promises. How so? When we trust in God as our Deliverer, He delivers us. Expressing faith in God as our Healer brings His healing. When we trust in Him as our Provider, He brings what we need.

Faith is different than hope. Hope is a desire that wishes to happen in the future. Think of faith as a present tense verb. Faith occurs now and it is something that we do. As we actively trust the Lord and stand on His promises, our faith will be released. Our shield will be in place.

1 John 5:4 says, "For whatever is born of God overcomes the world; and this is the victory that has overcome the world—our faith."

This scripture says if we are born of God, we can overcome "the world" (Satan's kingdom) by our faith in God.

We must have Jesus to have faith. Jesus is the author or creator of our faith. He is also the finisher or perfecter of our faith (Heb. 12:2). He begins it and makes it perfect.

I've restored antiques a few times, and I envision Jesus working on us sort of like that refinishing process. He sands our faith down, then polishes it, then sands it some more, then polishes it again…you get the picture.

We cannot have true spiritual faith that overcomes without Jesus. But with our faith shield that originates from Him, we can stop *all* the enemy's fiery missiles!

5) Our head is a vital part of our body that needs special protection. Our head encompasses the brain, which is the source of our intellect and driver of our personality. If we removed our brains, we would have no physical life.

Our head also houses the organs that let us see, hear, smell, and taste. Our physical senses impact our thinking and are especially vulnerable to attack.

We need special head armor to save us from the effects of the enemy. The helmet we are issued is called *the helmet of salvation* (Ephesians 6:17a).

Salvation refers to the act of saving. As we place Jesus as a protective covering over our head, He saves us from enemy's attacks aimed at our thoughts and senses.

Paul, in Romans 1:16, writes, "For I am not ashamed of *the gospel, for it is the power of God for salvation* to everyone who believes, to the Jew first, and also to the Greek." We don't get the full meaning Paul intended with our English words. In the original Greek, the word for salvation used here is *soteria*. Soteria means *rescue, or safety, deliver, health, salvation, save, saving.*[1]

God's salvation not only gives us life forever with Him, but also *delivers* us from the enemy *now*. Keeps us *safe now. Heals* us *now*. This is the full good news or gospel of Jesus Christ!

Jesus is our Savior. In Hebrew His name Yehoshua literally means "Jehovah is salvation."[2] Through Jesus we can be *saved from the effects of the enemy, now!*

I don't know about you, but I don't want to wait

until I go to heaven to receive His saving power, if I can have it now! Now is when we need it. Grab a hold of Jesus the Savior for your saving helmet armor.

6) Our last piece of equipment is the *sword of the Spirit,* which is the word of God (Ephesians 6:17b). The sword is a defensive weapon and also an offensive one. With it we can defend our territory (our homes, family, jobs, health, finances, etc.). We can also use it to go into enemy territory to take back what is rightfully ours. In other words, we can use the word of God to reclaim what has been stolen from us (health, finances, etc.).

We know the word of God is written as Holy Scripture. The following scriptures tell us how the Word of God is also Jesus.

> *In the beginning was the Word, and the Word was with God, and the Word was God.* He was in the beginning with God. All things came into being by Him, and apart from Him nothing came into being that has come into being. In Him was life, and the life was the light of men. And the light shines in the darkness, and the darkness did not comprehend (overpower) it.
>
> *And the Word became flesh, and dwelt among us,* and we beheld His glory, glory as of the only begotten from the Father, full of grace and truth. John 1:1–5, 14

Jesus' name before He became a man was "the Word." It is still one of His names. The mystery of Jesus as "the Word" is revealed a little further in Revelation 1:16, "And in His right hand He held seven stars; and *out of His mouth came a sharp two-edged sword;* and his face was like the sun shining in its strength."

The "two-edged sword" in this verse is the *spoken word that comes out of the mouth of Jesus the Word.* His words created worlds and defeated the most formidable foes.

"The Word" spoke to prophets, disciples, and teachers through the power of the Holy Spirit. They recorded His words, which we can read today as scripture. His written word still has all the power of its author, because in some mysterious way they are one and the same.

Jesus is "the Word." He is our sword of the Spirit. We have no weapon without Him. But with Him and His words, we can resist the enemy and win our battles!

Putting on Our Armor

By now you are probably saying, "All of this sounds great, but how in the world do I put my Jesus armor on?"

It's simple! We put it on with our words by faith. For instance, you could say, "I put you on, Jesus, as my full armor, that I may be able to stand against the schemes of the devil. Thank you, Jesus, that you are my armor of protection against the enemy." Then keep on going through each piece of armor, putting them on with your words by faith. Then trust and believe that Jesus is your protective covering. He becomes your armor as you say He is, and trust in Him to become it.

> *Put on the full armor of God,* that you may be able to stand firm against the schemes of the devil. For our struggle is not against flesh and blood, but against the rulers, against the powers, against the world forces of this darkness, against the spiritual forces of wickedness in the heavenly places. Therefore, *take up the full armor of God,* that you may be able to resist in the evil day, and having done everything, to stand firm. Ephesians 6:11–13

Part II—Maintaining Our Relationship

Speaking the word of God is of huge importance in our lives, but unless we know the One who wrote it, it's like holding a bazooka without instructions on how to use it. Not very effective.

Our protection and power originates from our relationship with our Lord and Savior. When we spend time with Him, our relationship develops. He not only becomes our armor, but more importantly, He becomes the love in our lives.

Who, What, Where?

First of all, just where is God, anyway? Matthew 3:2 says, "The kingdom of heaven is at hand." That means right here!

Most people believe God is somewhere "way up there." They think He doesn't get involved in the daily details of our lives. And they don't think He wants to become intimately involved with them.

It *is* pretty incredible to think that the most intelligent, powerful being, who created the universe, wants to have a close loving relationship with each one of us! But believe it or not—*He does and He will, if we'll work at being available to Him.*

[Moses said,] "But from there you will *seek the LORD your God, and you will find Him if you search for Him with all your heart and all your soul"* (Deuteronomy 4:29).

Who the Lord Is—Worthy

I am sure you must be a wonderful person. But until I really know who you are, I can't properly appreciate you.

That's how it is with the Lord. To know and truly appreciate our Creator, we first need to know who He really is.

The Hebrews have many descriptive names for our God that reflect His personality and tell us a lot about Him. He is:

Jehovah Elohim—the Eternal Creator; Self-Existent

Jehovah Jireh—the Lord will See and Provide

Adonai Jehovah—the Lord our Sovereign; Master

Jehovah Nissi—the Lord our Banner

Jehovah Ropheka—the Lord our Healer

Jehovah Shalom—the Lord our Peace

Jehovah Tsidkeenu—the Lord our Righteousness

Jehovah Mekaddishkem—the Lord our Sanctifier

Jehovah Saboath—the Lord of Hosts

Jehovah Shammah—the Lord is Present

Jehovah Elyon—the Lord Most High

Jehovah Rohi—the Lord my Shepherd

Jehovah Hoseenu—the Lord our Maker

Jehovah Eloheenu—the Lord our God

Jehovah Eloheka—the Lord thy God

Jehovah Elohay—the Lord my God

El Shaddai—the All-Sufficient One

El Olam—the Everlasting God

Qanna—Jealous (He wants our love and attention and doesn't like it when we give it to others more than to Him!)

We'll probably never in a lifetime be able to discover all that He really is. But when we start to grasp that He is each one of these names to us, at least we can begin to understand why we should honor and glorify Him with praise and worship.

If that wasn't enough to convince you, check out these

other names and titles that are designated to God the
Father, Son, and Holy Spirit:

Abba

Almighty Comforter

Alpha & Omega

Ancient of Days

Anointed One

Balm of Gilead

Beautiful

Beginning & End

Bridegroom

Bright Morning Star

Brook of Kidron

Brother

Christ

Counselor

Crucified One

Daystar

Deliverer

Door

Emmanuel

Everlasting One

Father

Friend

Gate

God

Good

Healer

Holy One of Israel

I Am

Jesus

King of kings

Lamb of God

Life

Light

Lord of lords

Messiah

Mighty God

Most High

Omnipotent

Omnipresent

Omniscient

Prince of Peace

Rabboni

Redeemer

Reigning King

Risen Lord

River of Life

Rock of Ages

Savior

Second Adam

Son of God

Son of Man

Teacher

Tree of Life

Truth

Way

Wonderful

Word of God

Word of Life

YHWH

Can you think of some more? I challenge you to study the names of the Lord and what they mean in the word of God. You'll discover the fullness of whom the Lord really is and what He wants to be in your life.

You might want to buy or borrow a good concordance of the Bible and use it to uncover the rich heritage that we have as children of the King. All that He is and all that He has, He wants to share with us.

In discovering who He is, we see that He is *worthy* to be exalted above all things. *As we get to know each part of His personality, He can become those things to us.*

The Psalms show us beautifully many of the characteristics of our Lord. He is our *rock*, He *trains* our hands for war, is our *loving-kindness, fortress, stronghold, shield* in whom we take *refuge*, and who *subdues* those under us (Ps. 144:1–2).

The Lord is *near* to all who call upon Him in truth (Ps. 145:18). He is our *help* and our *hope*. He *keeps faith* forever, *executes justice* for the oppressed, *gives food* to the hungry and *sets* the prisoners *free*. The Lord *opens the eyes* of the blind and *raises up* those who are bowed down. Our Lord *loves* the righteous, *protects* the strangers, and *supports* the fatherless and the widow, but He *thwarts* the way of the wicked (Psalm 146:5–9).

The Lord is our *keeper* and our *shade*. He will *protect* us from all evil, will *keep* our souls, and will *guard* us in all that we do (Psalm 121:5, 7–8).

The Lord is *good* and we are blessed when we take *refuge* in Him (Psalm 34:8).

Some of His benefits are: He *pardons* all our iniquities, *heals* all our diseases, *redeems* our lives from the pit, *crowns* us with loving-kindness and compassion, *satisfies* our years with good things so that our youth is *renewed*. The Lord is *compassionate* and *gracious, slow to anger,* and *abounding in loving-kindness* (Psalm 103:1–5, 8).

In Psalm 91, the Lord promises that when we *love Him* and *know His name,* He will *deliver* us and *set* us securely on high. When we call upon Him, He will *answer* us. He will *be with us* in times of trouble and will *rescue* and *honor* us. He will *satisfy* us with long life and will let us *see His salvation* (vs. 14–16).

Once we know who the Lord is *because of His name,* then we have the beginning of an understanding that should lead us to His throne in wonder and glory. Our Lord God is awesome and all fulfilling!

We worship Him in spirit and truth (John 4:24), for *He is spirit and truth.* We love Him with all of our hearts, for *He is love* (1 John 4:8). Finally, we honor Him with our praises and thanksgiving for He is worthy!

[The twenty-four elders in heaven say,] *"Worthy art Thou, our LORD and our God, to receive glory and honor and power;* for Thou didst create all things, and because of Thy will they existed, and were created." Revelation 4:11

A Holy Sacrifice

By now I guess it's pretty apparent the Lord is worthy of praise. But that doesn't necessarily mean we do it. We might be busy—or tired—or irritable—or not even see the need for it. But He *lives* in our praises (Psalm 22:3)! So sometimes, especially if we're not in the mood, we have to make a sacrifice and praise Him anyway.

I don't know about you, but I have a painfully hard time giving up something or not getting what I want. But sometimes I know it's for the best. That's a sacrifice.

Sacrifice means to give up something of value for a higher object or goal. When we offer up a *sacrifice of praise, we are giving of our time and emotions.* Whenever we don't think we have time, and when we don't feel like praising, is when it's the greatest sacrifice!

Hebrews 13:15 says, "Through Him then, let us *continually offer up a sacrifice of praise* to God, that is, the fruit of lips that give thanks to His name." We will turn from turmoil to rest, and from defeat to victory as we thank Him and praise His holy name.

Praise and worship is not an option for soldiers in the Lord's army. It's as important to our lives as drills are to a soldier in training. Praise helps to develop strength and grace in our spiritual muscles.

Without praise we'll flounder around outside of the Lord's presence and wonder why we live defeated lives. With it we'll enjoy His unmerited favor, mercy, protection, and love!

Postures of Worship

I had always heard the word "worship" relating to church services, but I came to understand what worship really means from a man named Norvel Hayes. I was listening to some of his colorful and entertaining stories on tape and could visualize the story he unfolded…

Norvel went with some students to a college campus to do some evangelical work. They were outside in a public area with students walking by. Some of the kids stopped to talk with him and through the course of conversation wanted to know what worship was.

In response, he simply knelt down on the sidewalk in his expensive business suit and lifted his hands up to the Lord. He closed his eyes and started saying to the Lord, "I worship you…I worship you…I worship you." He kept that up for awhile and as a result the power of the Lord fell on the group powerfully. As a result, some kids gave their lives to the Lord that day.

I could just visualize the humbleness and complete surrender of pride that allowed this millionaire businessman to physically show these young people how to worship right out in public regardless of his surroundings.

Through his telling of this poignant story I began to see what worship really is. It required abandoning the care of what other people thought about him. It required surrender. It required knowing the Master or wanting to know Him. More than anything it required the desire to express love, adoration, and appreciation for his Creator.

I was impressed with Norvel Hayes' unashamed explanation by example—and never forgot it. With this touching picture in my mind and heart, I began to study worship. What it is. How people do it.

I discovered there are various *postures* of worship that you can use at different times:

- Sing for joy in the Lord (Psalm 33:1).

- Give thanks and praise with musical instruments (Psalm 33:2).

- Sing to Him a new song (Psalm 33:3).

- Clap your hands (Psalm 47:1).

- Shout to God with a voice of joy (Psalm 47:1).

- Lift up your hands in His name (Psalm 63:4).

- Bow or kneel before the Lord (Psalm 95:6).

- Give thanks and call upon His name (Psalm 105:1).

- Sing praises to Him (Psalm 105:2).

- Glory (boast) in His holy name (Psalm 105:3).

- Seek the Lord's face continually (Psalm 105:4).

- Remember His wonders which He has done (Psalm 105:5).

- Praise the name of the Lord (Psalm 148:13).

- Be glad in our maker (Psalm 149:2).

- Rejoice in our King (Psalm 149:2).

- Praise His name with dancing (Psalm 149:3).

- Exult (leap up) in glory (Psalm 149:5).

- Sing for joy on our beds (Psalm 149:5).

There are as many ways to praise as there are people, for each person approaches the Lord in their own unique way.

Psalm 95:6 says, "Come let us *worship and bow down; let us kneel* before the Lord our Maker." Bowing and kneeling are terrific, but they don't work very well in the shower! Lifting up our hands to the Lord is a beautiful reaching out expression, but is not a very good idea while we are driving!

I like to raise my hands when I am worshiping the Lord. My husband says I'm raising my antenna. I think he's right!

Some postures are more comfortable for us than others, but you may want to use different ones as the Holy Spirit prompts. A soldier is only successful in battle if he is willing to use *different techniques for changing circumstances.*

The Lord made each one of us with different talents and abilities. He wants us to use them for His glory. If He has blessed you with the ability to play a musical instrument, play to Him. If you can sing, sing to Him of your love and thankfulness. When all else fails, shout joyfully, clap your hands, or simply raise them before Him in total adoration.

A spontaneous outpouring of our love and appreciation is all that's needed to constitute real praise and worship.

Attitude of Gratitude

I sure like it when my children have the right attitude! Our Father is looking for hearts with the right attitude. Psalm 100 gives us an idea how we should come into the Lord's presence...

> Shout *joyfully* to the LORD, all the earth. Serve the LORD with *gladness;* Come before Him with *joyful* singing. Know that the LORD Himself is God; It is He who has made us, and not we ourselves; we are His people and the sheep of His pasture. Enter His gates with *thanksgiving,* and His courts with *praise.* Give *thanks* to Him; *bless* His name. For the LORD is good; His loving-kindness is everlasting, and His faithfulness to all generations. Psalm 100

Our Father desires our complete love above all things. He wants us to *come into His presence with joy and thanksgiving. With love and praise on our lips.*

Imagine with me for a minute that you are head over heels in love with someone. The person that you love is so happy when they see you they shout for everyone to hear, "I love you! There is no one like my love!" They even sing songs to you and compliment all of your attributes!

Pretty nice to imagine, isn't it? Even if it would make

you feel silly, you would still be flattered and appreciative of their devotion. You would like their *attitude*.

An attitude of glad thanksgiving is what our Lord is looking for. After all, isn't He worth it?

Our Path or His?

If we're heading in the right direction with the Lord, we want to be in the middle of God's perfect will or desire for us. When we are living and doing what He has called us to do, we are inside His hedge of protection. When we are off doing whatever we want to, even if it's a good cause, we step off His path and consequently His protection.

When you hear the word *sin,* what does it bring to mind? I grew up associating guilt, condemnation, and just generally being bad with sin. Lying, cheating, stealing, murdering—you know, the Ten Commandment stuff! Then I graduated to thinking that sin is doing anything that separates us from God. I was getting closer.

As I was preparing a Sunday school lesson one afternoon, I was impressed to look up the meaning of the word "sin" in Hebrew and Greek.

The Hebrew word for sin is *chattath,* meaning "an offence and its penalty." It is derived from the root word *chata,* meaning "to miss."[3] The Greek root word for sin is *hamartano* or "to miss the mark." The derivative *hamartia* can be translated "a falling away from or *missing the right path*."[4]

I got the full picture one morning during a prayer time

in our church's chapel. I very clearly (in my mind) saw Jesus get up from a sitting position in front of the altar, turn, and begin to walk away. In my mind I anxiously said to Him, "Wait! I'm not ready!" He did not turn around but kept on walking.

A light went off in my brain. I wasn't supposed to ask Jesus to come walk with *me* every day. I was supposed to ask Jesus where I was going with *Him.* I had to take His path—not mine—if I wanted to stay with Him. If I weren't with Him, I would be missing the right path.

How often do we sin? The Greek and Hebrew definitions would suggest that we sin every time we get off the path where Jesus is walking. The verse "For all have sinned and fall short of the glory of God" (Rom. 3:23) takes on new meaning!

Not many of us lay down our own agenda each day and give the Lord a blank time schedule for Him to fill in. Pretty scary thought, isn't it?

I decided this was probably a new lesson the Lord wanted me to learn, so I began trying to follow Jesus each day. At first, foreboding thoughts flooded in like, *He'll just have you praying and going to see sick people in the hospital all day long and you won't have time to take care of your family and work.* I was nervous about what to expect, but I also knew that following Jesus was my heart's desire.

So in my quiet time with the Lord each morning, I began asking Him, "What are we going to do today?" I would get mental images of Jesus doing various activities— working in the yard, going with me to work, or sitting at the computer. I decided to do what I saw Jesus doing in my mind's eye. Throughout the day, I would continue to ask Him, "Where are we going now?" or "What are we going to do now?"

One time when I was behind in my writing schedule, I asked Jesus, "What now?" knowing full well that He was going to be at the computer. Surprisingly, I saw a picture of myself rubbing my husband's tired and aching shoulders and knew that was what I was supposed to do. He knew my husband needed to be ministered to and needed my hands to do it.

I found that following Jesus wasn't hard or out of the ordinary. It was actually a relief to receive and follow His direction, because it came with a sense of peace and a feeling of rightness. Try it and you'll see what I mean.

This way of walking with Jesus isn't hard, but it's a *habit* that has to be developed. Then we can say like Ruth did to Naomi, "Where you go, I will go" (Ruth 1:16).

Our Position with Christ

When we follow Christ's lead, we receive a spiritual position of honor and authority. Amazingly, in our kingdom of heaven, we are *seated with Christ* (Eph. 2:6). He gives us a position in the kingdom *above* principalities and powers. He wants us to take our position with Him and receive the benefits that He *died* to give us.

As we take our position with the Lord by faith, we are afforded His protection. Touching on Psalm 91 again, we see what His protection gives us:

Deliverance from traps and deadly sickness (vs. 3),

protection from the terror of the night and the missiles that are launched at us in the day (vs. 5), protection from sickness and destruction (vs. 6), no evil will befall us nor will any plagues come near our homes (vs. 10), He will give His angels charge concerning us to guard us in all our ways (vs. 11), and we will be able to tread upon the enemy (vs. 13).

Our Father created us to have a free will and wants us to choose to take our position with Jesus and receive His love and protection. But we don't have to. We can go on our merry way and do what we want to do. And be at the mercy of the enemy. The choice is ours.

If we choose to take our position with Christ, we will receive authority, benefits, and power. But with that position also comes an expectation of certain behavior. We're expected...

- to love,

- to forgive,

- to give without expecting payment in return,

- to take care of one another,

- to invest wisely what has been given us,

- above all, to reverence whom He is.

Great position requires great behavior. Challenging, isn't it?

Spend Time

More than anything, our Lord wants us to spend time with Him, loving Him. Usually, when we first begin spending time with the Lord, He listens quietly while we do all of the talking. In my experience, sometimes when we seek Him, it seems as if He "hides His face" or doesn't respond to us (Psalm 143:7). I think He waits to see if we are *serious* about our desire to spend time with Him. Then finally when we pass the waiting test, He begins to reveal Himself in profound and mysterious ways.

When I first began seeking the Lord, I naively expected immediate gratification, like a baby. I would go before the Lord with praise and thanksgiving like the scripture says to do and expect to "feel" the Lord's presence at the very least!

The Lord let me do that for weeks before I realized that I wasn't supposed to be spending time with Him for what He could do for me, but for what I could do for Him!

When my attitude changed to that of a loving, adoring child to her parent, things began to change. As I began to spend time ministering to Him in songs, words of praise and worship, and just simply loving Him, he began to reveal things that I never knew before.

The exciting and beautiful truth is when we seek Him, love Him, and give Him our attention, He returns that love in full measure.

In the days and months ahead, we'll need that personal relationship to guide us through tough times. Most people wait until disaster comes to fall down on their face before God and cry out to Him. Then we are so distracted by the circumstances that they overcome us instead of the Jesus in us overcoming the circumstances.

A little lesson the Lord gave me when I was preparing for children's church says it all…

I asked as usual, "What do You want me to teach the little ones this week?" One word came to my mind, "*Esther*." I read the book of Esther and then asked, "What do You want Your children to know about Esther?"

As I waited in the quiet, I heard in my spirit, "*The story is about trust and surrender—faith and love. Tell them this: Even as little Esther, a woman, trusted the king, so must you trust in God for answers to your prayers. But first you must do things that are pleasing to Him, so that in your time of need He will be pleased with you and answer your petition quickly.*"

We aren't above the children in needing to do what is pleasing to the Lord, but even more than that He wants our hearts. Not just dutiful work, but *the desire to do what is pleasing to Him because we love Him so much!*

CHECKLIST

1) Have you put on your *armor* by faith today?

2) Did you put up your *shield of faith?*

3) Do you have the *word of God* in your mouth—your *sword?*

4) Are you aware of our *enemy?*

5) Have you *worshiped* and *spent time with the Lord* today? Was it enough to really enjoy Him?

Fellow soldiers, these basics are the beginning of a march to victory:

- *The presence of Jesus living in and through us,* which comes by invitation and ongoing submission to Him. When we are full of His power, His triumph can become a reality in our lives. (If you haven't invited Him to live in you, now is a great time to do it!)

- *Familiarity with the word,* so we have a better idea of the Lord's viewpoint and can use it in times of need. That means read it until we remember it and then read it some more!

- *Recognizing who our enemy is and how they can try to come against us,* so we can resist with the word.

- *Worshiping and spending time with the Lord daily.* As we experience Him, we'll have clearer direction of the way He wants us to go. When we have *His* direction, we will be heading into *victory!*

Are we ready? *Onward!*

CHAPTER 2

KEEP YOUR EYES ON THE LORD

Our Inner Eyes

One crisp October Sunday, a famous tightrope walker instructed his new students to focus on an object across the room. As they focused, they were told to stand on one leg. The eager students obeyed their teacher without question. While standing on one leg, the pupils were then instructed to close their eyes. Like dominoes, everyone began falling onto one another amid shouts and laughter. Fortunately, they weren't on a tightrope that day.

Tino Wallendo drove home his point as he graphically illustrated what happens when you lose your focus. Without an object to focus on, it becomes almost impossible to keep your balance. He explained that when we can't see our goal, we fall short of achieving our destination. This is a vital concept in our walk with the Lord.

Seeing the Lord with our spiritual eyes is our first goal. Our eyes need to be on our Leader to receive his direction and instruction.

I had difficulty "seeing" our Leader at first and couldn't seem to connect with Him. Finally, I asked the Holy Spirit to help me "see" Jesus, as I should with my inner "eyes." From that time on, when I expectantly look for Him, I get a picture of Him in my mind. Sometimes I only see His face or feet or arms. Other times I just have an impression He is there.

Your picture of Jesus is a beautiful beginning point in your communication with Him. However He appears to you will be as unique as your relationship with Him. When you see Him with your spiritual eyes, He becomes a person to reach instead of a vague form "way up there." He is waiting expectantly for you to look to Him.

The wonderful blessing is when we focus on the Lord we see victory! There is no one and no thing that can defeat the Creator of the universe. With our focus on the Almighty One in charge, we can have confidence knowing no obstacle is too big for Him to overcome.

Part I—Miracles Can Happen

Trouble happens. It's just part of life. But what do we do when bad things happen?

Before I made Jesus Lord of my life, I decided what I wanted to do and when I wanted to do it. I liked it that way. Don't you? I would still like to "have it my way," but I've learned it isn't always the most prudent course of action. I would be sunbathing and eating chocolate chip cookies instead of writing this book if I was doing what I wanted to do...and getting fat and wrinkled instead of sharing a few good tips on beating the enemy at its game. It sure didn't feel natural, turning over the control to the Lord!

If we want to win our battles, it's prudent to let God call the shots. I learned a lot about what we should do in spiritual warfare from a story out of 2 Chronicles 20. The story is about a king named Jehoshaphat who was faced with an impossible situation. He was surrounded on all sides by his enemies and was looking at total annihilation. And we thought we had problems.

This story has an underlying lesson to teach us. It's a pattern or model to show us what to do in troubled times. It shows us the wonderful victory we can expect when we turn the control over to the Lord. Let's do a little Bible study and check it out.

> And Jehoshaphat was afraid and [1] turned his attention to *seek the Lord*; and [2] *proclaimed a fast* throughout all Judah. So Judah gathered together *to seek help from the Lord*; they even came from all the cities of Judah *to seek the Lord*. 2 Chronicles 20:3–4

As you see here, the king decided to seek help from the Lord by proclaiming a fast and asking all in the kingdom to join with him in prayer and fasting.

The next thing Jehoshaphat did, was to stand in the assembled people and implore God to move on their behalf…

> "Should evil come upon us, the sword, or judgment, or pestilence, or famine, we will stand

before this house and before Thee (for Thy name is in this house) and [3] *cry to Thee* in our distress, and Thou wilt hear and deliver us.'"

"O our God, wilt Thou not judge them? For we are powerless before this great multitude who are coming against us; nor do know what to do, but [4] *our eyes are on Thee.*" 2 Chronicles 20:9, 12

As Jehoshaphat and his people waited expectantly for the Lord's direction, the Spirit of the Lord came upon Jahaziel, and he relayed the Lord's instruction to the people...

> And he said, "Listen, all Judah and the inhabitants of Jerusalem and King Jehoshaphat: thus says the LORD to you, 'Do not fear or be dismayed because of this great multitude, for the battle is not yours but God's. Tomorrow go down against them. Behold, they will come up by the ascent of Ziz, and you will find them at the end of the valley in front of the wilderness of Jeruel. [5] *You need not fight in this battle; station yourselves, stand and see the salvation of the LORD on your behalf, O Judah and Jerusalem.'* Do not fear or be dismayed; tomorrow go out to face them, for the LORD is with you." 2 Chronicles 20:15–17

When they heard the Lord's faithful reply, they responded spontaneously with thankful joy and fell down and worshiped the Lord...

> And [6] *Jehoshaphat bowed his head with his*

face to the ground, and all Judah and the inhabitants of Jerusalem fell down before the LORD, *worshiping the* LORD. And the Levites, from the sons of the Kohathites and of the sons of the Korahites, [7] *stood up to praise the* LORD *God of Israel, with a very loud voice.* 2 Chronicles 20:18–19

Out of trust and obedience, the people acted on the Lord's word in faith, and they trusted Him and thanked Him in advance...

And they rose early in the morning and went out to the wilderness of Tekou; and when they went out, Jehoshaphat stood and said, "Listen to me, O Judah and inhabitants of Jerusalem, [8] *put your trust in the* LORD *your God, and you will be established. Put your trust in His prophets and succeed."*
And when he had consulted with the people, he appointed those who sang to the LORD and those who praised Him in holy attire, as they went out before the army and said, [9] "*Give thanks to the* LORD, *for His loving-kindness is everlasting."* 2 Chronicles 20:20–21

There was no doubt in the hearts of the people as they lifted up thankful praises to the Lord their Deliverer.

And when they began singing and praising, the LORD set ambushes against the sons of Ammon, Moab, and Mount Seir, who had come against Judah; so they were routed. For the sons of Ammon and Moab rose up against the inhabitants of Mount Seir destroying them completely, and when they had finished with the inhabitants of Seir, they helped to destroy one another. 2 Chronicles 20:22–23

Judah saw her enemy routed after *no fighting* on their part. They simply praised the Lord and trusted in His goodness.

When Judah came to the lookout of the wilderness, they looked toward the multitude; and behold [10] *they [there] were corpses lying on the ground, and no one had escaped.* 2 Chronicles 20:24

What the enemy meant for harm, the Lord changed to good when His people turned to Him totally trusting in His deliverance.

And when Jehoshaphat and his people came to take their spoil, they found much among them, including goods, garments, and valuable things which they took for themselves, more than they could carry. And they were three days taking the spoil because there was so much. 2 Chronicles 20:25

The Lord's people didn't forget who had saved them. They responded with honor, dedication and thanksgiving…

Then on the fourth day they assembled in the valley of Beracah, for there [11] *they blessed the*

LORD. Therefore they have named that place "The Valley of Beracah" until today. 2 Chronicles 20:26

What a tremendous miracle took place when God's people turned to the Lord and put their trust implicitly in the only One who could save them.

Can you imagine if our president called a fast throughout the land and every man, woman, and child went before the Lord and cried out to Him? Do you suppose we would see spectacular miracles like Jehoshaphat and his people did?

A Battle Plan

Did you notice the Lord addressed Judah, the *inhabitants of Jerusalem,* and King Jehoshaphat? Over and over in the scriptures, the word "Jerusalem" is used not only to mean the city, but also figuratively to mean citizens of the City of God. That's us, folks! So in scripture when we see "Jerusalem," it is important to look beyond the surface story and see what the Lord is telling us about the citizens of His kingdom.

A pattern for success was given in this story. When faced with dire circumstances, God's people:

1) decided to *seek* the Lord,

2) proclaimed a *fast,*

3) *cried out* to the Lord,

4) *placed their eyes on the Lord* and *expected an answer,*

5) *received direction* from the Lord,

6) fell down before the Lord and *worshiped,*

7) stood up to *praise* with a very *loud voice,*

8) put their *trust* in the Lord,

9) began *singing* and *praising* and *giving thanks* for the *victory,*

10) beheld the *enemy slain,*

11) they *blessed the Lord.*

Isn't it amazing that when they began singing and praising and giving thanks, the Lord set ambushes against their enemies? And then not only did He completely destroy the enemy, but He also left behind a tremendous blessing! It took them three days to move all of the valuables, because there was so much. And there was *no fighting!*

When we turn to the Lord with our whole heart and believe and trust in Him to deliver us, He will not fail us! He is faithful and true. We get into trouble when we look at the circumstances and allow them to overwhelm us with doubt and uncertainty.

This takes us back to what we see with our inner eyes. When we look to the Lord and trust in Him for the victory, this is the *eye of faith.*

The Jehoshaphat Kind of Faith

Jehoshaphat's story shows us faith in action. Jehoshaphat sought the Lord. He obviously believed his only hope for deliverance was a divine miracle sent from the Almighty Himself.

He was serious about getting an answer. He and everyone else involved in the situation set aside a time for fasting (self-denial) and cried out to the Lord for direction. He then set his eyes of faith on the Lord and expected and believed the Lord would show them what to do.

Seeking the Lord is serious business. It is not something we flippantly enter into. He is the most supreme being in the universe, and He expects us to be reverent, humble, and patient.

He will answer us if we believe that He will and if we wait on His timing. The waiting is where most people fail.

At a board meeting for the circle leaders in our church, the president of our newly formed group wanted to get us talking and decided to give us an "ice-breaker" activity. She posed the thought provoking scenario, "Imagine you were asked to pray about something very important. You prayed a long time. How long did you pray?" Almost without exception, five, ten, or fifteen minutes was a long time to pray for these women. And they were dedicated leaders in the church!

What would your answer be?

Proverbs 8:17 says, "I love those who love me; and *those*

who diligently seek me will find me." Diligence means to work hard and steady. We will find Him if we are willing to work at it. He will answer our questions, guide and direct our paths, and fellowship with us in incomparable joy and fulfillment if we will only seek Him with all of our heart.

Jehoshaphat waited and listened until he got his answer from the Lord. Then he obeyed the instructions to the letter. There was *no doubt* in his mind the Lord had prepared the victory for him and his people.

The Heartfelt Response

Jehoshaphat's people had faith in God's answers. Out of a spontaneous, thankful, and believing heart, the people responded with praise and worship.

Praise changes our hearts and drives out all fear—*because* the Lord lives in the praises of His people (Psalm 22:3). It is no wonder the hand of the Lord moved against the enemy when His people began singing, praising Him, and thanking Him for His loving-kindness.

No matter what instructions the Lord may give us, we need to respond with a heart of praise and thanksgiving. Praise Him exuberantly. The louder and more enthusiastic we become in our praise the faster His joy comes. With joy comes the assurance that the victory is already won!

Part II—A Look at Faith

What Is Faith?

When you were a child in school, did you sprout a bean and watch it grow? Faith is like the planting cycle. You plant a seed under the ground. You can't see it, but it's definitely there. When it receives the proper amount of water and sunshine and the soil is sufficiently warm, the seed germinates and up comes the plant.

When we plant apple seed, we get apple trees. When we plant corn, we get corn plants. If we plant tomato seed, we won't get cucumbers. Elementary, right?

The same thing happens when we plant the "seed" of God's word in the "soil" of our heart. Healing "seed" (scripture) produces healing. Deliverance "seed" gives us deliverance, etc.

We have *assurance* the seed will produce a plant after its kind. That belief and trust in God and His word is faith.

Hebrews 11:1 says, "Now faith is the *assurance* [*substance*—KJV] of things hoped for, the *conviction* [*evidence*—KJV] of things not seen." In the unseen world of God's kingdom, the things we hope for become evident *first* in the unseen spiritual kingdom (like the seed under the ground—you can't see it, but it's really there), *then* in the world we can see with our eyes. We believe God has granted our request *before* we see it with our natural eyes. Without belief that it is beginning to occur now in the unseen world, there is no substance or evidence to our faith. Hope says, "I'll have it sometime." Faith says, "I have it *now* even though I can't see it yet."

It's kind of like when David was called to be the new king of Israel. He was anointed by Samuel to be the new king a long time before his kingship was made apparent to the world. He was king from heaven's perspective, but from the world's perspective, it didn't happen until they saw it.

That's how it is with faith. Things we are trusting God for are already beginning to take place in the spiritual world around us, although we may not see them in the natural realm yet.

Jesus said, "Therefore I say to you, all things for which you pray and ask, believe that you *have received them,* and they shall be granted you" (Mark 11:24). Notice the *receiving* comes *after the believing.* In Matthew 9:29, Jesus said, "Be it done to you *according to your faith.*" We believe, then we receive.

We need to trust in what God and His word says— *more* than what we see and feel. Faith in God and His word says, "If God says it, then it is *true.*"

Faith Is Built on the Word

We can hear the word and not understand what it means. That doesn't do us much good, does it? We have to understand it to have faith in it and apply it to our lives.

Romans 10:17 says, "So *faith comes from hearing,* and *hearing by the word of Christ.*" Jesus used the word "hearing" many times in His teaching. He wasn't talking about just a physical response. He meant actually listening and *perceiving* what was being said.

Have you ever asked a child to clean up a mess? Sometimes I tell my children to clean up their rooms, and I know good and well they heard me, but they don't always respond. When they have really heard, they get to work.

In order to build our faith, we must first *understand* what the word is saying. The Pharisees "heard" the teachings of Jesus, but they didn't understand them and apply them to their lives. The hearing stopped at their ears and didn't get down into their spirits to make a change in their lives.

To build our faith we have to get into the word of God and *read* it, *listen to teaching* that is full of it, *study* it, and *pray* for the Holy Spirit to guide us into all truth concerning it.

As we incorporate the word into our heart so it becomes a part of our lives and actions, we will be able to see the fulfillment of God's promises that He gives His children. That's means you and me!

Part III—The Power of the Word

Speak the Word

In the church I grew up in, I remember being encouraged to pray silently. Looking back, I wonder why. Maybe there were too many of us for everyone to pray out loud. It could have been that it was a more private era or our church wasn't bold in the area of prayer. But whatever the reason, the leaders were the ones who prayed out loud.

Now I find that praying out loud seems to bring results quicker than praying silently. I'm not saying silent prayer doesn't accomplish anything, because it does. But when we confess out loud what the word of God says, our faith is boosted, and God responds to our faith in Him.

By speaking the word of God, we start a chain reaction, because *God's word always succeeds in the matter in which it was sent* (Isaiah 55:11).

Let's look at what happened when the disciples *spoke* the word that had been given to them.

> So then, when the LORD Jesus had spoken to them, He was received up into heaven, and sat down at the right hand of God. And *they went out and preached everywhere, while the LORD worked with them and confirmed the word by the signs (attesting miracles) that followed.* Mark 16:19–20

This scripture says Jesus was in heaven seated at the right hand of the Father while He worked with the disciples to bring forth miracles. The miracles that occurred were a direct result or confirmation of the word that was preached by the disciples. Isn't it exciting to know the Lord proves His word to be true with attesting miracles! He does this by showing us results *after* the word is *spoken.*

"Word" as it pertains to Jesus in the first chapter of

John means "logos" in Greek. Logos means "something said."

Jesus created, taught, healed, and delivered by speaking. It doesn't say anywhere in the Bible that Jesus prayed silently over people. He spoke to them. Jesus' disciples used His words to do the same and Jesus confirmed the words with miracles that followed. We should speak His words and expect miracles to happen in our lives.

Years ago, I entered a dry spiritual season that felt endless. I wasn't hearing from the Lord, my prayers weren't getting answered, and I felt like God was somewhere far away. I had a strong desire for Him and yet I couldn't seem to get through.

I shared my frustration with my friend Ann, and she reminded me of the verse, "And they overcame him because of the blood of the Lamb and because of *the word of their testimony*" (Rev. 12:11a). She reminded me the word *testimony* means more than telling about your experiences. It means literally "a statement used for evidence or proof."

I woke up and realized that if I were going to overcome, it would be through Jesus' blood *and my statement* of the word.

Armed with this revelation, I asked for the Lord's guidance, looked up all the scriptures I could find pertaining to relationship with the Lord, and claimed them to be mine. I kept saying the verses over and over during the day and night, and within twenty-four hours I felt renewed, strengthened, and full of the Lord again.

The Lord followed His word with an attesting miracle—His manifest (felt) presence!

Which "Word" Should We Speak?

What happens if we choose the wrong scripture to stand on for our problem? Is that possible?

Most faith teaching I hear indicates that we are supposed to find a scripture for our circumstance, then claim it and believe the Lord will honor His word with a confirming miracle. Sounds good, doesn't it? There are a lot of wonderful teachers helping people to build their faith with this concept (they sure helped me), but are they leaving out the most important part?

When we *seek the Lord first*, we can know the proper paths to follow, scriptures to stand on, and right decisions to make. When we ask Him what we should do in our circumstances, then He has a chance to guide us.

The problem is we want to make the decisions! When my youngest daughter was little, she used to tell me, "I want to do it myself!" If Kaitlin were the boss, she would eat candy for breakfast, stay up until midnight, and would consequently be sick and tired. When I am in charge, she eats what is good for her and gets enough rest.

The same is true in our relationship with our heavenly Father. He knows what's *better*, even when we think we know what's best.

For example, which of the following verses would you choose if faced with a crisis? "Submit therefore to God. *Resist the devil* and he will flee from you" (James 4:7), or the opposite, "You need not fight in this battle; station yourselves, *stand* [*stand still*—KJV] *and see the salvation of the Lord* on your behalf, O Judah and Jerusalem" (2 Chron. 20:17).

The first verse indicates the need for action on our part, and the second states no action is necessary. Neither of these is right nor wrong, but offer two *different solutions* to problems. It can make the difference in winning or losing our battles if we stand when we should be resisting, or if we resist when the Lord wants us to be still.

When it comes to "the word," no one knows it better than the one who spoke it. Ask Him to guide you to the verse or verses that are most appropriate for your problem. Then follow the inner prompting of the Holy Spirit.

A Promise

In 1985, I was reluctantly preparing for knee surgery. I had torn the cartilage in my right knee six years earlier, and it had become gradually more painful until I couldn't bear it any longer.

The choice to have the cartilage removed had been a difficult one, because the doctors informed me that to remove the cartilage would eliminate the pain now but would guarantee arthritis in the knee at some future point in my life.

With incessant pain gnawing at me night and day, I decided to give in to the surgery.

At this point in my life I didn't know God's promises, but I believed that God could heal us if, and only if, He wanted to. So the weekend prior to my scheduled surgery date, I asked my parents, brother, and his wife to pray for my healing. That prayer changed my life.

As we gathered together in the warm familiarity of my parent's living room, I settled down on the couch and waited for them to pray a simple little prayer for my knee to get well. What happened instead, to my amazement, was they laid their hands on me and began to pray. My brother's voice lost its Southern drawl as the Lord began to speak unforgettable words to me through him. He spoke to me about several things in my life and then said, "*I will give you the miracle of the healing of your knee if you will but have faith, patience, and obedience.*" There was more, but these are the words that will stand out in my mind for the rest of my life. I wept, but the tears were joyful, for the Lord had reached down and taken the time to speak to me.

From that moment on, I made Jesus LORD of my life. I decided that if He was talking, I was listening.

Just prior to this, my parents had started attending Full Gospel and other Christian conventions. I couldn't understand for the life of me why. After all, wasn't it just teaching about salvation from sin? Little did I know they were learning about *faith* and the *promises of God* and *miracles that happened as a result.* In my limited understanding I thought they were listening to boring preachers give condescending lectures, but in reality they were being fed the *life* that is in the word of God.

Fortunately for me, my father bought all the teaching

tapes from these conventions, and boy, did he load me up with them after this encounter!

There were tapes, tapes, and more tapes of faith teaching and healing messages. I *heard* the word. I *believed* it. I *acted* on it.

I learned that like the seed as it prepares to sprout, there could be a time when my knee was actually healed in the unseen world of God's kingdom, but the manifestation in the physical world that we see and touch would not have occurred yet.

Timidly, I began to stand in faith for my healing, and I nervously but expectantly canceled the surgery.

One of the chief scriptures that I felt led to use during this time was Mark 11:22–25:

> And Jesus answered saying to them, "Have faith in God. Truly I say to you, *whoever says* to this mountain, 'Be taken up and cast into the sea,' *and does not doubt in his heart, but believes that what he says is going to happen, it shall be granted him.* Therefore I say to you, *all things for which you pray and ask, believe that you have received them, and they shall be granted you.*
>
> "And whenever you stand praying, forgive, if you have anything against anyone; so that your Father also who is in heaven may forgive you your transgressions."

As a novice, I began to do what this passage says to do. I spoke to the "mountain." In this case, the "mountain" was the pain in my knee. All day and all night as I was alone and awake, I spoke to my knee. I quoted the scripture and said, "Knee, I call you well. I call you healthy and normal in Jesus' name. Pain, I call you gone. I call you removed in Jesus' name."

The Lord had told me to have patience, faith, and obedience, so I kept this up for months. Sometimes I could believe and the pain was less. Then I would waver and I would have more pain. My husband astutely observed, "It seems like your knee is a spiritual barometer for you." I reluctantly mused over this thought and decided to get more serious about receiving my healing. Nonetheless, eleven long months went by with the pain coming and going. One lonely night when my husband was out of town, I woke up with excruciating, throbbing pain in my knee. I sat up in bed and got *mad* at Satan for robbing me of my health. I yelled, "Satan, get your hands off of my knee. I will *not* receive your pain any longer. Be gone in Jesus' name!" Then I thanked the Lord for healing my knee once again, rolled over, and went to sleep. When I woke up the next morning, all of the pain was gone! Glory to God! And my knee is healed to this day.

I believe this eleven-month period was like the seed dormancy period. My faith was like the seed planted and I had to "water" it with the Living Water, which is the word of God.

It appears the lacking ingredient was kicking the enemy off his nest. The cloud has to be removed before the sun can shine through!

A word of caution. The enemy knows when you

speak with authority and when you don't. The key to that authority is to be sure you are full of the Holy Spirit. If you are an empty vessel, you have no power or authority. *The Lord in you is your authority.* It's not a good idea to try bossing evil spirits around without the power of the Lord residing in you!

Maybe you've tried what you thought was standing in faith but you didn't get an answer. Check it out...when you *doubt,* when you are *unsure,* and/or when you *wonder when* the Lord is going to bring forth the manifestation, there is no real faith. You may have hope—but not faith.

Faith is *believing, being sure of the outcome* and *knowing* the Lord is doing it *now!*

Eternal Rights—Legality or Reality?

Our eternal life doesn't begin when we go to heaven. It begins now! When we chose Jesus as our Lord and Savior, we began the beautiful journey of a never-ending relationship with Him. Our travel begins in a world away from our King's home, but we have the promise that he will transport us there when our bodies pass away.

Our eternal alliance and life with Jesus the King affords us certain rights and privileges right here and now, but those privileges don't help us very much if we don't know we have them.

When my oldest daughter Heather first got her driver's license, she hadn't learned how to drive yet. She had the rights and privileges of driving by law, but she hadn't learned the skills of driving a car. She had a driver's license, but it didn't do her much good until she learned how to drive.

The same principle applies to our eternal rights. We can have them "legally" as part of our citizenship in God's kingdom, but until we learn about them and use them, they don't do us much good.

"*Fight the good fight of faith; take hold of the eternal life to which you were called,* and you made the good confession in the presence of many witnesses" (1 Timothy 6:12). Learning about our rights that are due to God's promises is one thing. Overcoming doubt that it will really happen as the word says is another story. The good fight of faith refers to our struggle to overcome our doubts. Winning the fight of faith occurs when we trust and believe that God honors His word *every time when we believe it* and are not swayed by what we see and feel that's contrary to the word of God.

God is not a liar. His word is *truth.* Believe it. Stand on it. *Do not doubt,* and you will have the fulfillment of His promise!

CHECKLIST

1) Can you see the Lord with your *inner eyes?*

2) Before you begin to pray for a need or a special circumstance in your life, do you *seek the Lord* for instruction? How long do you *wait* for an answer? Have you tried *fasting?*

3) Do you *expect an answer* from the Lord?

4) When you receive your answer do you then begin *praising and worshiping* until you actually see the results in the physical realm?

5) When you see the results of the victory, do you *bless the Lord* from a heart of abundant thanksgiving?

6) Are you *studying the word* and asking the Holy Spirit to help you understand it?

7) Do you *believe what the word of God says* even more than what you see and feel?

It is vital in our walk with the Lord that we have new "manna" or spiritual food each day. It is absolutely critical that we have correct direction. Without Jesus as our daily guide, it's too easy to step off the path He is leading us on.

If we try to guess which promise to appropriate or how to respond to a set of circumstances, we could choose incorrectly. We need to maintain our relationship and *seek His guidance in all things.*

Above all, we need to *see* the Lord with eyes of faith. He will perform miracles in our lives and provide indescribable fulfillment. And He'll radiate out of us and perform signs and wonders as a witness to the world.

The beauty of being in the Lord's army is, the Head Chief not only gives instructions to the top generals, but all the way down to the lowliest private.

Have you received your orders today?

CHAPTER 3

THE MAKING OF MIRACLES

Are you willing to follow the instructions of the greatest miracle worker of all time? You may be in for some surprises!

[Jesus said,] "Truly, truly, I say to you, *he who believes in Me, the works that I do shall he do also; and greater works than these shall he do;* because I go to the Father. And whatever you ask in My name, that will I do, that the Father may be glorified in the Son. If you ask Me anything in My name, I will do it. *If you love Me, you will keep My commandments.*" John 14:12–15

Wow! How could we possibly do greater works than Jesus did? The following verses tell some of the commandments Jesus was referring to…

And He said to them, "Go into all the world and *preach the gospel* to all creation. He who has believed and has been baptized shall be saved; but he who has disbelieved shall be condemned.

"And *these signs* will accompany those who have believed: *in My name they will cast out demons, they will speak with new tongues; they will pick up serpents, and if they drink any deadly poison, it shall not hurt them; they will lay hands on the sick, and they will recover.*" Mark 16:15–18

Amazing! Are you ready for this kind of power? How are the followers of Jesus able to accomplish these incredible commandments? If you remember, Mark 16:19–20 talks about Jesus helping his disciples from heaven...

So then, when the LORD Jesus had spoken to them, He was received up into heaven, and sat down at the right hand of God. And they went out and preached everywhere, *while the LORD worked with them, and confirmed the word by the signs (attesting miracles) that followed.* Mark 16:19–20

Are you ready to follow His instruction, too? If your answer is yes, the good news is our commissioning comes with power!

When a father brought his possessed son to Jesus for deliverance, he asked Jesus "if" he could do anything to help... "And Jesus said to him, 'If You can!' *All things are possible to him who believes*" (Mark 9:23).

To *believe* is to actually be convinced that something is true or real. We as believers are convinced that Jesus is the only begotten Son of God and His teachings are *true.* When we are convinced His sayings, teachings, and commandments are true, we will base our lives on them and miracles will follow.

Part I—The Groundwork Is Prayer

Most Christians seem to understand the salvation from sin message pretty well, but I haven't seen the vast majority of Christian's stepping out into the deep waters of faith where miracles reside. Have you?

This deeper level of faith comes as a direct result of *time spent with the Lord.* In this quiet time we are refueled with the Holy Spirit who fills us with His power.

We need a prayer life like Jesus had!

A Quiet Place

"And in the early morning, while it was still dark, *He arose and went out and departed to a lonely place,* and was praying there" (Mark 1:35).

It is essential to *go into a quiet* (or "lonely") *place* to remove ourselves from the distractions in our busy lives. These distractions are what keep us from focusing on the Lord as we need to. They create interference in our "reception," or hearing from the Lord. The challenge is finding the quiet places and times to go before Him where there will be little or no interruption.

Is it as hard for you as it is for me to find that quiet time? Sometimes I have to get up really early before my family wakes up. Other times I have to get into the car to be alone and pray. Jesus didn't always pray in the same place, and we probably won't be able to either.

I can promise you the Holy Spirit can and will prompt us to pray at times that are unexpected. This sometimes requires sacrifice on our part. You may have to get out of the bed in the middle of the night and give up precious sleep. Our flesh groans and says, "Later, Lord," but later may be too late.

One Saturday evening not long ago, my mother called to ask for prayer for my father who felt pressure in his chest. He didn't want to go to the hospital, and he is such a man of faith, he was standing on the word of God and telling the symptoms to go away.

I went into the only quiet place I could find at that moment, the garage! I sat on the concrete steps and leaned back against the kitchen door and began to lift my father up to the Lord, asking Him how to pray. I immediately thought of my cousin Theresa, so I decided to call her from my "quiet place." We prayed what came to our minds and after awhile we gained a peace and a lighter feeling in our spirits. We both sensed my father had narrowly dodged a bullet.

I was incredibly tired after an entire day of cleaning house and working in the yard, but I felt very impressed to pray for my father in person...so off I drove to Gainesville.

Upon arriving at my parents', I didn't notice anything alarming about my father's condition, but was obedient to the impression to lay hands on my dad and pray. When I pray for others, I close my eyes, ask for the Lord's direction, and then pray what I "see." This time was no exception.

I could "see" a picture of my father in a wrestling match. Then I could see the wrestling match was over, but my father was lying on the ground worn out. Then I saw a mantel lain on my father's shoulders. A mantel of power and of supernatural wisdom and knowledge. I thanked the Lord for His mantel and prayed for my dad as the thoughts came to me.

When we were finished praying, I perceived that only my dad could win his wrestling match, but he could and would win by faith in God and His word. I shared this with him and we went to bed.

The next day my dad felt better, but still not great. I went into the only place I knew I could be alone to pray—the bathroom! As I sought the Lord, a very distinct thought came to me. As I continued to pray the thought came again and again. The thought was, *A check up is in order.* I shared that with my parents, and Monday my dad went in for a check up.

The doctors determined that over the weekend, my dad had a heart attack. He had two blockages that were very significant and would need bypasses due to their location. He also had a leaky heart valve they believed was a result of the damage from the heart attack. They wouldn't know if the valve would be operable until they went in for open-heart surgery.

To make this story shorter, my whole family prayed asking the Lord to make it clear to us and especially my parents whether he should have the surgery or stand in faith for his healing. Through a series of revelations, we felt very confirmed he was supposed to have the surgery. The bypasses were a success, and the leaky heart valve was healed by the time he went in for surgery!

So, if we are being impressed to pray, there is a reason for it. There may be a crisis looming, or it could be a test of our obedience. Go into the quietest place you can find and just do it! Someone's life could be at stake. The more obedient we are, the more we will be trusted with.

Pray Often

Jesus prayed *often*... "But He himself would *often* slip away to the wilderness and pray" (Luke 5:16).

Luke, led by the Holy Spirit, wanted us to understand that Jesus prayed more than once in awhile. He prayed *a lot*. He used that time to refresh and renew Himself for His tremendous ministry. And especially to enjoy spending time with His heavenly Father.

I have found the frequency of our prayer life has a lot to do with how "full" we seemed to be of the Lord. I picture it kind of like we're an automobile and our fuel is the Holy Spirit. No fuel, no supernatural power.

His "fuel" shines as the light of the Lord. When His fuel is in us, it shines out of us to others. His fuel is going out all the time. And when we minister to others, it's like stomping on the gas. If we're not careful to stay hooked up (in prayer) to His fuel line, we can run out of gas. It takes *frequent* "pit-stops" to stay fueled up and ready for our journey.

We need to pray—and pray often—for the working of miracles to be evident in our lives.

Prayer Keeps Us Out of Trouble

"And when He [Jesus] rose from prayer, He came to the disciples and found them sleeping from sorrow, and said to them, 'Why are you sleeping? *Rise and pray that you may not enter into temptation*'" (Luke 22:45–46). We are no different than the first disciples. Sometimes we wear out and give up.

So much has been said about Jesus' deity that I think we sometimes forget He was also human while He was on earth. He knew and felt human emotions. I'm sure He knew what it felt like to want to sleep a little longer. He was tempted in different ways just like we are (Luke 4:2).

The difference between Jesus and us is He pressed through and overcame temptation in spite of the circumstances. We can, too, when we have Jesus in our center of being. *He wants to help us overcome* our fleshly desires and temptations. For Him to help us, we need to decide to pray just like He did—alone and frequently.

He is calling us to *spend time* with our heavenly Father. He desires it. We need it. And we won't see many miracles coming forth from our lives without it!

Part II—Four Dynamics of a Miracle

#1—*Hope*

Every miracle begins with hope. Without hope there can be no miracle, for *hope is the desire of your heart*. To put it another way, hope is what you *will* or want to happen.

When the Lord made us, He put in us a free will. He gave us the power to choose so we would be like Him, not puppets. The tremendously hard thing to grasp is no matter what, *He will not make us do anything against our will*. Even if it kills us.

"And a certain man was there, who had been thirty-eight years in his sickness. When Jesus saw him lying there, and knew that he had already been a long time in that condition, He said to him, *'Do you wish to get well?'*" (John 5:5–6). Jesus asked the sick man if he wished or *hoped* to be well. He will not force wellness on us, even if it is for our own good! First, it must be our hope or heart's desire.

From hope, He waits for us to *believe* in Him as our Savior and Healer. As our hope turns into belief, the Lord *responds* to our trust in Him.

In summary:

- We hope
- We believe in Him for our need
- He responds

Within the boundaries of hope comes knowing *specifically* what you want. If you need healing in your right shoulder, then pray for that exactly. If you need a certain sum of money for a special need, then ask for exactly what you need.

When my son was around seven years old, he saved up his money and bought an exotic Asian turtle. He was very proud of his little turtle and took it everywhere with him for one whole day. So of course he took it with us when we went to visit his nana.

Nana lived in a picturesque courtyard condo only a few feet from the St. Johns River. Brenden decided to let the turtle have a little freedom and stretch his legs, so he let it crawl around the living room. Then he went outside to do a little exploring himself. When he finally remembered to check on his turtle, it was nowhere to be found. After searching frantically for what seemed like hours, we decided it must have made a straight line for the St. Johns River.

Brenden was absolutely devastated. As I sympathetically watched the little guy with his head hung low, I asked the Lord how to pray. For some unknown reason out of my mouth came, "I ask you, Lord, to send a turtle for Brenden right to our front door." Then I realized what I had said! I quickly prayed, "Lord, I don't know why I said that, but I thank you for fulfilling it!"

Would you believe that three days later I opened up the front door and a very large gopher turtle was on our front porch walking toward the front door! I excitedly called Brenden and he was thrilled to see his new-found pet. However, his joy quickly turned to concern when it refused to eat or drink. He came to the conclusion that turtles really need to live in their natural habitat, so he finally turned it loose in our large wooded back yard. And I thanked God for answering another prayer. Very cool, don't you think? A specific prayer was answered specifically.

The Lord wants to be our Provider, Healer, and Savior, but first we turn to Him. As we show Him our heart's desire, pray specifically and trust in Him, He fulfills the answer to our needs.

#2—*Faith*

From a specific hope we move into faith and patience. Let's look at how to turn hope into faith…

One time when I was seeking the Lord about what to teach my adult Sunday school class, He dropped a thought into my spirit that really made me stop and think, "Many never progress from *hope* into *faith*. You think you have faith, but there is a missing ingredient."

While I was pondering this idea, all of a sudden I saw a picture of the word *faith* with wings and feet attached! Then I saw a diagram with *hope* at the left side, and extending from it an arrow drawn to a picture of God. Then the picture became animated with someone praying or speaking words of hope for what they needed to God, and then God's answer came back full circle to them. *It wasn't until God gave an answer/direction in how to proceed that hope turned into the winged faith.*

I believe God wanted our class to know that our hopes do not turn into faith until we seek Him and He replies to us. Faith is trusting in God and His will—not our desires. We must know His will in our circumstances before true faith is released. Then we can stand in faith until we see the answer because we have an assurance from Him.

How can you know His will for the circumstance? First of all, it will *always* line up with scripture, and usually it will *be a scripture* that leaps out at you from memory or while studying or praying. Secondly, you should sense His peace about what you are supposed to do. A good rule of thumb is if you don't have peace about it, don't do it! We'll talk more about how to hear God in a later chapter.

When we have and believe God's promise, and trust in Him to bring it about in our lives, then our faith is released. When our faith is released, then God begins to bring forth the promise first in the unseen spiritual world, then in the world we see.

Let's look at Hebrews 11:1 again because, if you're like me, you can read this verse over and over and still not quite grasp the full meaning. "Now faith is the *assurance* of things hoped for, the *conviction of things not seen.*"

Assurance means to make sure or certain. Conviction is the state of being convinced or a firm belief. In other words, faith *makes sure of* things hoped for and is the *firm belief* of things not seen.

It is with our firm belief that we make sure of our hope coming to pass. This is the substance of faith. Without faith we might not see our hopes turn into miracles.

When I am standing in faith for an answer to prayer,

it helps me to visualize it as if it had already happened. I "see" it completed. This helps me not waver in spite of the circumstances.

Since faith is the "firm belief of things not seen," we need to remember that "firm belief" means just what it says. Doubt, wavering or wondering *when* it is going to happen, is going to negate our firm belief.

> But *let him ask in faith without any doubting*, for the one who doubts is like the surf of the sea driven and tossed by the wind. For let not that man expect that he will receive anything from the LORD, being a double-minded man, unstable in all his ways. James 1:6–7

When our son was six years old, he developed a painful growth on the side of his heel, which we decided was a small plantar wart. Our choices were we could either take him to the doctor to have it "frozen," or let God remove it. Our son elected to let God do it since He is a painless surgeon!

This was the desire of his heart, but dear old mom wanted to help God with it. We asked Jesus our Healer to remove the wart and then I would apply a salicylic acid patch to the growth. The acid patch was my idea. I thought it wouldn't hurt to help things along. We kept this up for several months as the growth kept getting larger and more painful.

When my husband put his foot down and said Brenden would have to go to the doctor to remove the wart, I realized we better get serious about letting God do His work or to the doctor we would go!

I began to see my acts of applying the acid patches really said, "I don't trust You to heal my son as quickly as I want You to. I'm going to help hurry it up." In effect I was not really trusting God. I wanted to take matters into my own hands. But I was learning when Jesus is Lord of our lives we better trust it all to Him.

With newfound insight, we went before the Lord again. This time with humbleness, trust, and belief that He needed no assistance from meddling mom! After receiving God's direction, we by faith placed the cleansing blood of Jesus over the growth, cursed its roots (like Jesus cursed the fig tree that bore no fruit, Mark 11:20–25) and thanked Him for healing my son's foot. Every night after that my son prayed his own special little prayer, "Thank you, Lord, for killing the stupid, dumb, dead growth and making the stupid, dumb, dead wart go away."

We became very excited as each day the growth became smaller and smaller until all that was left was a slight scar where it had been.

I realized anew what a fine line there is between faith and unbelief. The Lord expects us to trust Him *totally* and without *any* kind of reservations. He is looking for an unwavering firm belief.

Does this mean that we quit going to the doctor and taking medicine? After I first heard the faith messages concerning healing by the power of God, I felt guilty about ever seeking assistance from the medical profession.

Finally, I went before the Lord and asked Him how and/ or if we should use medical help.

He reminded me that Jesus is the great Physician. He can't stand to see His people dying and sick for lack of knowledge, so He gives us help in the way of physicians and medicine to help fill in for our lack of faith and knowledge. He clearly showed me they are a very special people, because they are healers like Jesus is a healer. We are to appreciate people in the medical profession for their work and dedication to help alleviate suffering.

The Lord may guide you to use the medical profession from time to time. He may use them to fulfill His plans and answer our prayers. And it helps tremendously to know exactly what to pray for, which comes after a proper diagnosis.

When we are sick, the most important thing is to ask the Lord *how* He wants to heal us, and what He wants us to do. As we seek Him for guidance, He'll impress upon us the right course of action and give us His peace concerning it.

If your faith in God and knowledge of His word isn't sufficient to believe in big miracles, start with the small ones that you *can* believe for. The Lord gives us basic blocks to build our foundation of faith with before He starts adding the first, second, and third floors!

If we're wounded or weak, it can be so hard to get our faith up to where it needs to be—*unwavering*. So call in the back-up troops! That's what we're here for. Battles aren't normally won with a single soldier, are they? The

Lord wants His army united and supporting each other in all we do.

When we pray with someone who is spiritually stronger than us, it helps build our faith until it rises to the level we know beyond a shadow of a doubt He is answering our prayers *now*.

#3—*Patience and Endurance*

When we are waiting on the Lord to enact the desires of our heart, many times He calls us to be patient. He has His perfect timing and doesn't change it for you or me or anyone else. As I have heard said about the Lord before, He is neither early nor late, but always right on time. That is *His* time!

Even if we know all the right scriptures and have received direction from the Lord, it doesn't mean that He is going to fulfill a promise right this minute. He might, but then again right now may not be appropriate for His purpose. So then we wait on Him.

But we don't want to wait! So why do we have to wait? (1) Sometimes the Lord has a lesson for us to learn while we are waiting. (2) Maybe our faith in Him falls short of what He is expecting. (3) Frequently He waits for the events that He is orchestrating to come about before He enacts His miracle. (4) There may be spiritual warfare that delays our answer.

When the waiting isn't due to lack of faith, we need to remember that some seeds take longer to sprout than others. It doesn't mean they are not germinating, just the conditions have to be right to produce the plant.

Don't give up even if you don't see the answer to prayer after days, weeks, months, or even years. The Lord *will* fulfill His promises.

Will we continue to wait and believe through the test of time? The Greek word for endurance used in James 1:3–4 is *hupomone*. Which means cheerful (or hopeful) endurance, constancy, patience, patient continuance (waiting).⁵ What can we possibly gain from cheerful, hopeful, patient waiting?

> Consider it all joy, my brethren, when you encounter various trials, knowing that the testing of your faith produces endurance [patience—KJV]. *And let endurance have it's perfect result, that you may be perfect and complete lacking in nothing.* James 1:2–4

The Holy Spirit through James tells us to be joyful when our faith is tested! He tells us the testing of our faith produces patience, which is the ability to bear trials without grumbling. I still have a long way to go on that one!

I heard a teacher say the Lord showed her she was like a pressure cooker. He reminded her it's the pressure of steam that tenderizes what's in the pot. When she "vented her steam" by complaining, it took a lot longer for what was cooking (her soul) to get tender. Her "release valve" was supposed to be venting to God—not complaining to others.

If you're like me, patience is hard! But it's encouraging

to see the promise contained in this passage. We will *lack in nothing* when we have *patience,* through the *testing of our faith.*

How is our faith tested?

- Through *time* (having to wait is so hard!)

- through *overwhelming circumstances* (the problem looks too big)

- through *lack of knowledge* (we don't have enough word in us to stand on)

- through *fear* (the enemy loves this one)

- and the list goes on.

Any of these is enough to bring on doubt. What should we do when that happens?

"We are destroying speculations and every lofty thing raised up against the knowledge of God, and *we are taking every thought captive to the obedience of Christ...*" (2 Corinthians 10:5). This says we have to destroy "speculations" or ideas that are raised up against what we know to be true of God and *take every thought captive* that is contrary to what Jesus expects from us.

Taking every thought captive is a pretty tall order, but I find that by repeating this verse and telling Jesus that I am bringing Him my thoughts and laying them at His feet, *doubt flees.* Putting His blood (with my words, by faith) over my mind helps a lot, too.

The enemy can't stand the word of God or the blood of Jesus. Use them. Remember the word of God is the sword of the Spirit, and the blood of Jesus protects us.

The Lord wants us to be battle-ready. Don't forget to use your sword and put on your protection! Then wait on the Lord with *patience.*

#4—*Love*

Love is a part of every miracle, for out of our Lord's heart comes an abundance of love and compassion for His people. *His miracles are a product of His love.*

> Beloved, let us love one another, for love is from God; and everyone who loves is born of God and knows God. The one who does not love does not know God, *for God is love.*
>
> By this the love of God was manifested in us, that God has sent His only begotten Son into the world so that we might live through Him. In this is love, not that we loved God, but that He loved us and sent His Son to be the propitiation for our sins.
>
> Beloved, if God so loved us, we also ought to love one another. No one has beheld God at any time; *if we love one another, God abides in us,* and His love is perfected in us. 1 John 4:7–12

The love of God is a higher kind of love than we are accustomed to giving. It is an all-giving, all-forgiving love.

Can you imagine sacrificing your precious son who is always good and kind and never does anything wrong, for other children who are constantly getting into trouble?

Can you fathom the love that will *always* forgive every nasty thing that we can possibly think of doing? This is God-love.

When the Lord lives within you, His love wants to reach out and touch other people's lives. When we allow His love to pour through us, it is unselfish, pure, and holy. He is calling us to this kind of love for the making of miracles.

> If I speak with the tongues of men and of angels, but do not have love, I have become a noisy gong or a clanging cymbal. And if I have the gift of prophecy, and know all mysteries and all knowledge; and if I have all faith, so as to remove mountains, but do not have love, I am nothing. And if I give all my possessions to feed the poor, and if I deliver my body to be burned, but do not have love, it profits me nothing.
>
> *Love is patient, love is kind, and is not jealous; love does not brag and is not arrogant, does not act unbecomingly; it does not seek it's own, is not provoked, does not take into account a wrong suffered, does not rejoice in unrighteousness,* but *rejoices with the truth; bears all things, believes all things, hopes all things, endures all things. Love never fails...*
> 1 Corinthians 13:1–8a

As I have mentioned before, unless we are full of the Lord, we have no real power. It is the power and the love of God working *through* us that enables us to deliver His gifts of miracles. We are His hands, feet, and mouth to the world at this time, but unless we are filled with Him, we can't share what He has to offer.

God is love and His love is perfected in us as we love one another. To love one another at all times with the God kind of love is not something we will be able to do in our strength. We rely on the Lord to flow forth from our lives as an outpouring of our relationship with Him.

That outpouring is all the things that Christ is: *love, healing, compassion, strength, joy, truth, salvation, provision, faithfulness, sanctification, righteousness, and peace* to name a few! We simply can't be that perfect without Him, but with Him all things are possible.

The New Testament tells us the Lord's hand moves in response to compassion for His people. That compassion stems from His depth of love for us. It is that love that unfolds miracles.

> [Jesus said,] "A new commandment I give to you, that you *love one another, even as I have loved you,* that you also love one another. By this all men will know that you are My disciples, if you have love for one another." John 13:34–35

Our Lord commanded us to love one another. If we're holding a grudge against someone or believe that someone has wronged us, we must forgive them. If we feel that poor or dirty people are not quite up to our standards, love them anyway. Jesus does.

I have a friend named Marilyn who shared a humbling experience with me. She was in church sitting in a pew, feeling very holy. A dirty, smelly, homeless person came in and sat next to her. She was uncomfortable wishing he would move a little downwind when the Lord clearly spoke to her, "His stench is on the outside, but yours is on the inside." Wow! She realized then that none of us is better than another.

When we sacrifice our pride, anger, or whatever is holding us back from being a pure vessel the Lord can use, His love can flow and His miracles will come forth!

Part III—Ways the Lord Heals

He Wants to Heal Us—Get Rid of Sin

We had an employee one time named Wanda. She loved to tell people with a gleam in her eye that her name was "Wicked Wanda." She enjoyed her wicked ways!

The Old Testament is not only rich with promises the Lord gives to His faithful people, it is also quite specific about the consequences of evil and wicked action, and of *true* repentance.

> If I shut up the heavens so that there is no rain, or if I command the locust to devour the land, or if I send pestilence among My people, and *My people who are called by My name humble themselves and pray, and seek My face and turn from their wicked ways, then I will hear from heaven, will forgive their sin, and will heal their land.* 2 Chronicles 7:13–14

Our heavenly Father disciplines to get our attention and focus back on Him where it needs to be, then rewards our correct behavior with forgiveness, healing, and reconciliation.

Throughout the Old and New Testaments, we find the Lord revealing His true nature to us. He tries to get us to respond to His depth of love and commitment with a similar feeling of loyalty and dedicated love. It is through that *reciprocal relationship* the Lord's full measure of blessing takes place.

The Lord wants to see us all saved, healed, and holy, but not every person will yield to Him. Many times sin in our lives *that we don't want to let go of* can hinder us from receiving what He wants to give us.

What if we have a sin we like? Pride was my pet sin. I don't think I had a humble bone in my body and I enjoyed it! I was critical of others and thought I was right—at least most of the time!

For years it was a battle for me to keep placing my pride on the Lord's altar as a sacrifice. It seemed like pride would keep bubbling up from within me. I had people pray for me, and I prayed asking the Lord to deliver me from it for years.

Finally, one Wednesday night at a Vineyard Church service I got more than I bargained for. As the sweet sounds of praise and worship faded away, a man in the front spoke out, "There is a fire burning tonight. It will sweep through..." That's all I remember because a woman up front started sobbing loudly. I thought, *That's strange,* because I was feeling pretty cheerful!

Then all of a sudden the Holy Spirit moved in me and I began crying uncontrollably. I really wasn't sad and didn't feel a lot of emotion, but my body was wracked with sobs. I thought, *This is really weird.* Then behind me I heard someone else start crying. I heard one after another began crying and sobbing. From the sounds of the sobs, it sounded like the Holy Spirit was moving in a circular pattern around the congregation…then around again…then around again and again. In my heart I asked the Lord, "What are you *doing?*" Immediately I heard in my spirit, "*Burning pride out of you.*"

This unusual phenomenon continued until I was worn out, so I sank to the floor and kept on crying. I was surprised and yet somewhat comforted when someone draped a lightweight cloth over my head. I was told later they called it a "prayer shawl." I appreciated the limited privacy it afforded me as deep, wrenching sobs continued to tear from my body. As I resigned myself to the purging, I could hear similar sounds all around me, and I realized the Lord was working on many of us. Nearly two hours later I felt the heaviness lifting from me. As suddenly as it started, I quit crying and timidly peeked out of the shawl and looked around the room. Most of the people were sitting on the floor and were just starting to dry their eyes as well.

Man, what a humbling experience! I think I was baptized by fire that night (Matt. 3:11–12). And gratefully, I don't seem to have problems with pride anymore.

> And He [Jesus] was saying, "That which proceeds out of the man, that is what defiles the man. For from within, out of the heart of men, proceed

the evil thoughts, fornications, thefts, murders, adulteries, deeds of coveting and wickedness, as well as deceit, sensuality, envy, slander, pride and foolishness. *All these evil things proceed from within and defile the man.*" Mark 7:20–23

Sin hinders our relationship with the Lord and has a detrimental impact on receiving from Him.

Do you have any "pets" that need to be sacrificed?

We Are Disciples, Too

Remember that miracles came forth from Jesus' first disciples *as a direct result of preaching the gospel.* This good news spoke not only about receiving eternal salvation, but also salvation from evil, today.

When we choose to put behind sin and spiritual death to join the kingdom of light, we are supposed to sit, walk, and stand *with* Jesus, through the Holy Spirit. If we are with Jesus, our position is *above* other spiritual powers and manipulations of the enemy.

When we take our place by His side and are certain of His victory over *all* the works of the devil, then we are ready to perform His works among His people.

[Jesus said,] "*If you abide in Me, and My words abide in you, ask whatever you wish, and it shall be done for you. By this is My Father glorified, that you bear much fruit, and so prove to be My disciples.*" John 15:7–8

We are His disciples today. By following the example of the first disciples, we can know we're carrying out Jesus' direct orders as He gave them before He ascended into heaven. They walked and talked with Him and knew beyond any doubt that what He said and did was true. We need to believe and act like they did—*full of trust in Him and His word.*

Prayer and Praise

We may not have been beaten and thrown into prison lately for the work of the Lord, but many people are in a spiritual prison and don't even know it. Paul and Silas, in spite of wrongfully being in prison, prayed and sang praises to the Lord.

> But about midnight *Paul and Silas were praying and singing hymns of praise to God,* and the prisoners were listening to them; and suddenly there came a great earthquake, so that the foundations of the prison house were shaken; and immediately all the doors were opened, and everyone's chains were unfastened. Acts 16:25–26

Praise is an important weapon in our warfare. *It changes our hearts.* It replaces our despair with hope, joy, and victory!

I had a precious little lady help me with my housework for several years during a rough period in my life. Sometimes I would be in tears when she got to my house, and Rosa would put her short, plump arms around me and say, "We need to stomp on them devils!" She took me by the hand and had me stomp around the room with her. She would yell at the devil and tell him he was under our feet! Then we would start laughing and giggling, and the joy of the Lord would start to well up in us. Then she kept on stomping around the room yelling, "Praise the Lord!" and I followed her lead. We got pretty happy, pretty quick. To be honest, I felt pretty silly doing it, but we sure saw results.

I encourage you to try marching around the room yelling, "*Praise the Lord!*" for a while and see what happens. You might feel silly at first, but the enemy would like to keep you from praising, so don't listen to any ideas that would keep you from doing it. Just try it. After you quit giggling, you'll be amazed!

When I was at a Benny Hinn conference in Orlando, we sang a lot of praise and worship songs, and then people started coming up to tell of the miracles that happened to them during praise and worship. One after another came forward to tell their story of healing that came *during* praise. I found it interesting there wasn't any preaching before the miracles of healing started popping up.

The next day I realized some delayed speech problems I had been suffering with as a result of an accident were greatly improved. I had not gone to the meeting seeking healing, but the Lord gave me a special touch that night.

I'll say it again. *The Lord inhabits the praises of His people* (Psalm 22:3). Praise Him all the time and enjoy watching Him *move*.

His Word

Believing the words of Jesus is essential in the working of miracles. Once, a royal official whose son was sick to the point of death, went to Jesus and asked Him to go to his son to heal him. He believed the words of Jesus...

> The royal official said to Him, "Sir, come down before my child dies." Jesus said to him, "Go your way; your son lives."
> *The man believed the word that Jesus spoke to him* and he started off. And as he was now going down, his slaves met him, saying that his son was living. So he inquired of them the hour when he began to get better. They said therefore to him, "Yesterday at the seventh hour the fever left him."
> So the father knew that it was at that hour in which Jesus said to him, "Your son lives"; and he himself believed, and his whole household. John 4:49–53

Faith in what God speaks to you brings forth miracles. As I've said before, when we are so sure in our hearts that what He said is truth, there is *no doubt* that it is more true than anything we can see or feel. In other words more true than our circumstances.

The enemy may try to come against us with symptoms of sickness and disease, with poverty and any other awful thing you can think of. But if it is contrary to what God and His word says—*it is a lie!* Think about it. If it isn't truth, then what is it? A lie!

Here is how I discovered that truth...

One time I developed a painful sore throat, and having nursed my kid's through their childhood illnesses, I knew it was strep. It tasted like strep, it looked like strep, and it smelled like strep. Ew!

As usual, I prayed and asked the Lord if I should go to a doctor. I saw the words in my mind's eye, "It is a lie." I wasn't quite sure what to do with that.

I went to my brother's house that afternoon and asked him what he thought about that word. With his usual direct insight he said, "Well, if it's not the truth, it's a lie, isn't it?" How simple and yet profound!

With newfound revelation I could stand in faith on God's assurance the symptoms I experienced were a lie and not His truth. We started calling the sore throat a lie and calling it gone in Jesus' name. In a few hours, it was gone!

To be effective against the enemy we need to be continually feeding ourselves truth from the word. My friend Eleanor advises that to read a chapter in the Bible each day is a great goal, but if all else fails, read at least one verse!

It is vital to get the living water (the word) in us or we will dry out. It is our nourishment. When we read it, we are fed spiritually.

As abstract as it may seem, *the written word is alive to our spirit.* It is alive because it is a part of Jesus.

> For the word of God is *living and active* and sharper than any two-edged sword, and piercing as far as the division of soul and spirit, of both

joints and marrow, *and able to judge the thoughts and intentions of the heart.* Hebrews 4:12

The words Jesus spoke through the Holy Spirit, both before and after He became flesh, are as much a part of Him as hair or skin. His words are the essence and very nature of Him. To receive them is to receive the life of Christ.

To have faith in God's word, we must *know it, believe it,* and *stand on what it says*—no matter what! Jesus always follows His word with attesting miracles (Mark 16:20). We need to understand and accept this and let it become our way of thinking, for faith in God and His word will bring forth miracles in our lives.

"*He sent His word and healed them, and delivered them* from their destructions" (Psalm 107:20).

Living Blood

We know Jesus' blood protects us. But faith in His living blood will also bring forth miracles in our lives.

You should be aware by now, the blood of Jesus was sacrificed for us to cleanse us and atone or make amends for our sin nature. The purity of it soaks up our guilt, absorbs and removes it from God's sight. It is only through His blood that we can be holy and acceptable to God our Father.

It is also through His blood the devil is rendered powerless.

Since then the children share in flesh and

blood, He Himself likewise also partook of the same, that *through death* [His shed blood] *He might render powerless him who had the power of death, that is, the devil;* and might deliver those who through fear of death were subject to slavery all their lives. Hebrews 2:14–15

And I heard a loud voice in heaven, saying, "Now the salvation, and the power, and the kingdom of our God and the authority of His Christ have come, for the accuser of our brethren has been thrown down, who accuses them before our God day and night.

"And *they overcame him because of the blood of the Lamb and because of the word of their testimony,* and they did not love their life even to death." Revelation 12:10–11

As we see in Revelation 12:11, "they overcame him [the devil] because of the blood of the Lamb *and* because of the word of their testimony." It took Jesus' pure, unblemished, and holy blood *and* speaking His word in appropriate application to overcome Satan. We need to use both of these weapons in our warfare of faith.

I heard a story about a family who lived in an area with rabid foxes. One of the family members went around the four corners of their property and said, "I place your blood, Lord Jesus, around the boundaries of my property as a hedge and protection." Within the next week they found several dead foxes just outside the boundary of the property, that tested positive for rabies.

When I heard this story, I decided it sounded like a great idea, rabid foxes or not. So I asked Jesus for His protection and stood in my home and faced each direction of our property and said, "I place your blood, Lord Jesus, as protection all around my property. I place your blood on the four corners of my property, and I declare no harm shall come to my property or my family or dwelling."

Our property is a heavily wooded half-acre lot in a residential area. We've gone through several hurricanes and have had small tornados and twisters come through our area. Several times the storms have snapped off trees right up to the easement on the rear of our property, but I am grateful the Lord's blood protected our property from damage each time.

How the blood of Jesus is applied to our lives is the same way we came into His salvation—by faith. His blood isn't something we physically touch and yet it is just as real as He is. And He offers it freely to us. The beautiful truth of His blood is:

- it never runs out—it is always flowing;
- it is always available—just as Jesus is;
- it cleanses us—soaks up sin;
- it protects us—the enemy is defeated by it;
- it heals us—makes us whole;
- it renews us—empowers us with His life;
- it is applied simply—with our words.

Even as Jesus is pure and holy, so is His blood. *Take* it

reverently by faith and use it to heal the brokenhearted, the weak, and the suffering. Joyfully *apply* it as a hedge of protection and covering of atonement. Gratefully *accept* its cleansing us from all unrighteousness. It is only through this reconciling covering that God the Father can receive us as pure and worthy of His presence.

Jesus shed His blood freely for us. Use it freely, with joy and thanksgiving for what He has done for us!

The Name of Jesus

Do names reflect and perhaps even create who we are as a person? Long ago, names were given to people to mean something. They selected names that said what they were feeling or even what they wanted to happen.

The Lord changed Abram's name to Abraham because He intended to make Abram the father of a multitude of nations. It was important that Abram's name be changed to reflect what the Lord was bringing forth through him. The name Abraham means literally "the father of a multitude." By changing Abram's name to Abraham, God was using His creative force of the spoken word to achieve the result He desired.

Jesus changed the name of Simon (shifty one) to Peter (a rock), to change his identity. Here again, the Lord used the spoken name to reflect the change He was bringing about in the man previously called Simon.

My name is a Hebrew word meaning "lily or pure." It also stands for a trumpet because of the shape of the flower. I laughed when I first found out what my name meant because nothing could have been further from the truth! Now I see the Lord has been working to line me up with my name. He's still working on it!

Jesus gave us permission to use His name with His authority, so the Father would be glorified through the Son.

> And whatever you ask *in My name,* that will I do, that the Father may be glorified in the Son. If you ask Me anything *in My name,* I will do it. If you love Me, you will keep My commandments. John 14:13–15

A great story in Acts tells us what can happen when we use His name. One day when Peter and John were on the way to the temple, a lame man began to beg them for money. Peter's response was better than money...

> But Peter said, "I do not possess silver and gold, but what I do have I give to you: *In the name of Jesus Christ the Nazarene*—walk!" And seizing him by the right hand, he raised him up; and immediately his feet and his ankles were strengthened. And with a leap, he stood upright and began to walk; and he entered the temple with them, walking and leaping and praising God.
>
> And on the basis of *faith in His name, it is the name of Jesus which has strengthened this man* whom you see and know; *and the faith which comes through Him* has given this perfect health in the presence of you all. Acts 3:6–8, 16

It was *faith in the name of Jesus* that healed the lame man. Remember, the name Jesus means literally "Jehovah is salvation." What a powerful name! To say His very name is saying the Lord God is our salvation.

It's important that Jesus' name means salvation, but it is even more important that our faith in *Him* be established for the working of miracles. Then we can use His name with assurance the "power of attorney" He gave us will be acted upon as He so clearly stated.

Know Your Master

How well do you know your Master?

A long time ago, a man named Paul knew Him very well. He had never seen Jesus in the flesh, just like we haven't. But Paul spent so much time seeking the Lord, he knew Him intimately and performed extraordinary miracles as a result.

Some other people heard of the miracles he performed and tried to copy what he was doing, and they were rudely awakened…

> But also some of the Jewish exorcists, who went from place to place, attempted to name over those who had the evil spirits the name of the LORD Jesus, saying, "I adjure you by Jesus whom Paul preaches." And seven sons of one Sceva, a Jewish chief priest, were doing this.
>
> And the evil spirit answered and said to them, "I recognize Jesus, and I know about Paul, *but who are you?*" And the man in whom was the evil spirit,

leaped on them and subdued all of them, and overpowered them, so that they fled out of that house naked and wounded. Acts 19:13–16

If we know our Master, the enemy will know us like they did Paul.

If we are afraid of what the enemy might be able to do to us, we shouldn't get into the miracle business. Lack of assurance of who we are in the Lord can allow the enemy to bring chaos and destruction.

When we are full of the Holy Spirit, there will be no contest as to who the winner will be in *any* confrontation with the enemy.

Be Humble and Yielded

Using the Lord's name with authority is a wonderful privilege that He gave to us as His disciples, but He cautioned that we are not supposed to get excited about the power.

And the seventy [disciples the Lord had appointed] returned with joy, saying, "Lord, even the demons are subject to us in Your name." And He said to them, "I was watching Satan fall from heaven like lightning. Behold, I have given you authority to tread upon serpents and scorpions, and over all the power of the enemy, and nothing shall injure you.

"*Nevertheless do not rejoice in this, that the spirits*

are subject to you, but rejoice that your names are recorded in heaven." Luke 10:17–20

It is really fun to see the Lord's power at work. However, keeping a humble and yielded attitude is part of our walk with Jesus. When we remember the biggest miracle is we are forgiven for all the junk we've done and are even adopted into "the holy family," that is something to get really excited about!

Pray and Anoint with Oil

Do you use cooking oil? Or machine oil? They're great for cooking and lubrication. But have you tried anointing oil?

Anointing the body with oil was a widespread custom in Middle and Far East cultures. Perfumed ointment was commonly used to welcome guests. Oils were both poured on and rubbed into the skin for moisturizing and cleansing. Consecrated oil was used for setting things apart for holy service.

The early disciples were thought to have used the finest olive oil for anointing. The oil would be blessed and set apart for anointing the sick and other holy tasks.

Is it outdated today to anoint people with oil when we pray for them?

Is anyone among you sick? Let him call for the elders of the church, and let them *pray over him, anointing him with oil in the name of the LORD;* and the prayer offered in faith will restore the one who is sick, and the LORD will raise him up, and if he has committed sins, they will be forgiven him.

Therefore, confess your sins to one another, and pray for one another, so that you may be healed. The effective prayer of a righteous man can accomplish much. James 5:14–16

Anointing with oil reaches out and touches someone. It combines our actions with the Lord's name. When these are offered up in faith we can expect the Lord to respond with restoration and forgiveness.

We as soldiers need one another. If we confess our sins to each other when we fall, the stronger soldiers can help pull us back up. When we pray for one another when someone is sick, the wounded soldier can be made whole again to rejoin the Lord's active army.

If the Lord impresses you to, don't be timid—anoint with oil. It is the *demonstration* of faith in action.

Lay Hands on the Sick

Jesus needs our physical hands to touch those with needs.

And it came about that the father of Publius was lying in bed afflicted with recurrent fever and dysentery; and Paul went in to see him and *after he had prayed, he laid his hands on him and healed him.* Acts 28:8

Paul followed Jesus' example and instruction to "lay

hands on the sick and they will recover" (Mark 16:18). But notice that before he ministered, he *prayed*. With fresh anointing and direction, he was full of the power of the Lord and could minister to the sick man.

We can't pour out of an empty vessel. First, we're filled with the Lord, *then* we put our hands on the sick—and let the Lord do the rest!

Don't worry about the possibility of not seeing the healing the moment we pray. Put pride aside and realize it is God's choice for the time and place the miracle happens. It may occur an hour later or even a year.

Our job isn't to wonder when the Lord's hand will move. Our job is to lay our hands on the people who come seeking the Lord and to allow the Lord to use us as His hands, if He desires.

He will use us if our attitude is one of humbleness and obedience to His word.

Prayer and Fasting

Being in the miracle business is living a prepared and "fasted" lifestyle. Jesus was in a prepared state to deal with whatever came before Him. But His disciples were not always ready for every situation.

> And one of the crowd answered Him, "Teacher, I brought You my son, possessed with a spirit which makes him mute; and whenever it seizes him, it dashes him to the ground and he foams at the mouth, and grinds his teeth, and stiffens out.

And *I told Your disciples to cast it out, and they could not do it."* Mark 9:17–18

Jesus rebuked the unclean spirit, telling it to come out and not enter him again. After it threw the boy into terrible convulsions, it came out and left the boy unconscious. Jesus took him by the hand and raised him up.

Later, when the disciples spoke with Jesus privately, they wanted to know why they couldn't cast out the evil spirit. Jesus replied, *"This kind cannot come out by anything but prayer [and fasting*—KJV]" (Mark 9:29).

Either we need to be prepared in advance (the wiser choice) or begin prayer and fasting when presented with some of life's more difficult challenges. Being a soldier in the Lord's army requires living a life of prayer and sacrifice.

In my experience, the Lord calls us to a fasted lifestyle more often than to a specific fast. Not self-indulgent, but givers of what we have. Sharing and sacrificing of our time, money, food, or whatever the Lord lays on our heart.

When we are very serious about getting an answer to a specific question or problem, fasting helps to quiet our body down enough to hear. When it's not telling us all the time, "I want...I think...I feel..." it's easier to hear what the Lord is saying.

Fasting all or part of our food for certain periods of time helps make our body obedient to our mind and spirit. After a while our body quits telling us what to do, and our spirit begins to be in control. Believe it or not, when we tell our body it isn't the boss anymore, it will actually settle down and be quiet. Sometimes it takes a few days though! Be persistent. It will happen.

The Lord responds to the sacrifice we offer Him in the spirit in which it is given. As we seek Him, He'll guide us to the appropriate sacrifice, and it will surprisingly be less painful than we're expecting!

Believe in Jesus

Do we believe in Jesus enough to tell others?

[The people that were following Jesus said] to Him, "What shall we do, that we may work the works of God?" Jesus answered and said to them, "This is the work of God, that you *believe in Him whom He has sent."* John 6:28–29

The early disciples taught the whole gospel of Jesus Christ because they had seen Him firsthand and believed in who He was and what He said. They believed and taught that through Jesus you can have *eternal salvation, wholeness, wellness, deliverance, and freedom from the bondage of sin.*

Let's spread the whole good news of Jesus and "believe in Him whom He sent" to be the real miracle worker. Then signs and wonders will follow our teaching, too!

CHECKLIST

1) Have you established a *prayer life* like Jesus'?

2) Do you have *hope* for your miracle?

3) Do you have *faith* and *patience* to see it through?

4) Do you have the *love* of God emanating from your life?

5) Have you truly *repented* of your "favorite" sin?

6) In spite of the circumstances, do you *pray* and *sing praises* to the Lord?

7) Do you believe the *word* of God is the highest truth? Are you full of it?

8) Is the living *blood* of Jesus a part of your life?

9) Do you use Jesus' *name* with the authority He gave you?

10) Do you *know your Master?* Is your attitude humble and yielded to Him?

11) Are you willing to *anoint with oil* and *pray* for the sick?

12) Will you *lay hands* on the sick and pray for them?

13) Are you willing to *fast and pray?* To live a fasted lifestyle?

14) Do you truly *believe* in the good news of Jesus? Are you willing to *teach* the whole good news?

The Lord calls us all to be miracle workers in His kingdom. Whether we serve our family, our church or the nations is not as important as our willingness to fulfill His tasks.

Come on! Let's serve Him by serving others in the kingdom.

CHAPTER 4

MY STORY

As a Child

I grew up in a family where the church we attended was our home away from home. It seemed every time the doors to our Southern Baptist church were open my mother made sure we were there.

Between choir practice, Girls' Auxiliary, Training Union, Sunday school, Sunday morning and evening services, and of course Wednesday night Bible study, when were we not there?

My mother taught little children in Sunday school, and my grandmother taught adult classes when they weren't teaching us. It's no wonder that my heart and mind were filled with Bible stories and scripture verses from an early age.

From a child's perspective, I learned wonderful stories about God the Father and His Son Jesus. As a result, I respected, loved, and admired my heavenly Father and felt very close to Him. I also understood in a simple way that Jesus had sacrificed His life for me so that I would be able to go to heaven when my body died. But in my young heart, Jesus was a hero figure, not a real person to know and love.

At the ripe old age of ten I made the decision to be baptized. I wish I could say it was because of a life-changing experience, but in reality I was afraid I would miss out on heaven if I didn't! Looking back, I see this naive beginning was the apparent start of a series of stepping-stones in my spiritual journey.

> And they were bringing children to Him so that He might touch them; and the disciples rebuked them. But when Jesus saw this, He was indignant and said to them, *"Permit the children to come to Me; do not hinder them; for the kingdom of God belongs to such as these.*
>
> "Truly I say to you, *whoever does not receive the kingdom of God like a child shall not enter it at all."* And He took them in His arms and began blessing them, laying His hands upon them. Mark 10:13–16

As a Teenager

From the lovely age of thirteen, I began seriously searching for who or what God was. Was He some big power like they described in Star Wars as "The Force"? Was He real? I took a class on comparative religions at my friend's Episcopal church and was left with more questions than answers. Which religion was really right? Everyone seemed to have a different answer.

Most of all, what I heard about Jesus had me completely

baffled. Why did people say they knew Jesus personally? After all, He was in heaven, wasn't He? How could you know someone personally that didn't talk back?

My mind was full of seemingly answerless questions, but a simple Bible verse my mother often quoted to us when we were growing up kept haunting me. "…ask, and it shall be given unto you; seek, and ye shall find; knock, and it shall be opened unto you" (Luke 11:9 KJV). To my surprise, as I sought and knocked, doors began to open up to me.

On the first day of school in my sophomore year at Gainesville High School, I noticed a couple of very interesting characters in homeroom. There was Cynthia, who dressed all in black and proclaimed to be a witch. But a boy named Herbie who looked like one of the "Three Musketeers" captured my attention.

As the bell rang, our teacher gave the normal first day of school instructions, to stand up, give our name, and briefly tell something about ourselves. When Herbie took his turn, I couldn't help but notice his dramatic attire. With his ruffled white shirt, tight black leather clothes, New York accent, and long black curly hair, he seemed to have stepped out of the pages of my history book. When he announced proudly he was a "Jesus-freak," I was totally dumbfounded. I had never seen anyone that nonconformist be so bold about Jesus! I was quietly eager to know more.

I was excited but nervous when several weeks later Herbie asked me over to the little house where he lived with some college-age Christians. He invited me in and sat on the opposite side of the small living room and began talking about Jesus. He asked a question that I had heard many times growing up, but had never really understood, "Have you ever asked Jesus to come into your heart?" Even though I had been raised in the church and baptized at an early age, I had to confess that I didn't know what that meant.

Herbie explained that Jesus is a real, living person that we can know, even though we can't usually see Him. He went on to say that in the Bible it clearly states that Jesus will respond when we invite Him to come into us to be our personal Savior.

The thought crossed my mind that in scary movies, people were possessed by evil spirits who lived in them. Would this be the opposite? I had learned enough about Jesus and God the Father as a child to know that if they lived in me as spirit beings, they would be a good and holy influence. I thought, *If He's alive and real, something wonderful could happen, and if He isn't, what could it hurt?*

Herbie kept on talking and sharing his testimony and I pretended to listen to him, as I inwardly thought about what he had just told me. It sounded so simple. If it was really that easy, why not try it?

Silently, I spoke to Him and said, "Jesus, if you are really there, I want you to come into my heart right now."

Within seconds I was flooded with an intensely peaceful floating sensation. With childlike awe, I discovered He was really real! Suddenly my mother's verse came to my mind, "Seek and ye shall find. Knock and it shall be opened unto you." Wow! This was getting good!

The holy euphoria I experienced in the Lord's presence stayed with me for several days until the world and all of its temptations caught up with me. My teenage willpower wasn't very strong, and I stepped out of the felt presence of the Lord by sinning. I was disappointed and yet strangely relieved, because the intensity of the power of the Lord felt overwhelming to me. Despite my relief I felt an immediate hunger for more of Him. I couldn't forget what I had experienced. My gracious, loving, heavenly Father had led me to His precious Son. And He was real and powerful!

The next stepping-stone in my spiritual journey came when I joined a Bible study group that Herbie introduced me to. The group consisted of around twenty people, ranging in age from high school to college. Our common denominator was a keen desire to know God. The Lord honored our innocent expectancy with answers, signs, and wonders that would cement our faith in Him and belief in His holy word.

One night at the Bible study, we studied about seeking the Lord. Our normal pattern was to ask God to show us what He meant by the scriptures we read, so this night we began silently praying and reaching out to Him, each of us in our own prayerful way.

After about thirty minutes of straining to reach contact with the Lord with all my spiritual might, these very distinct words were spoken loudly into my spirit, "*Stand up and go!*" My eyes flew open and I looked anxiously around to see if anyone else had heard the voice. Everyone was deep into prayer, and I realized the words had been spoken to me alone.

My heart beat wildly, and I didn't know what to do. My mind raced...it was a cold winter night...I would have to get up and walk through the group to retrieve my coat and Bible...then where was I supposed to go?

Panicking, I quickly said, "Let me have five minutes, Lord!" Then purposely erased the words from my mind and told myself I must have been imagining things. I intently began to pray for members of my family. I was in the middle of a request when all of a sudden (it must have been five minutes to the second) His voice interrupted my thoughts and said sternly, "*Stand up and go!*"

I was afraid to obey the voice, but I was even more afraid not to if it was really a direct order from God. So I shakily stood up, gathered my belongings and nervously walked out of the church sanctuary, with no idea where I was going.

As I entered the quiet vestibule of the church, I saw someone crouched on the floor shaking with uncontrollable sobbing. In that instant, I knew the Lord had called me out of the group to help this person in distress.

I put my arms around them and was immediately joined by a leader from the group. We talked and prayed, and the Lord I was beginning to know and love replaced their pain with joy and laughter. I wondered later, *What would have happened if I hadn't gotten up and left when I heard the voice tell me to leave?*

I don't know what I was expecting when I sought the Lord so intently that night, but it wasn't a loud voice! The awesomeness of it intimidated me so badly that I didn't seek the Lord with the same intensity again for fourteen years.

Another time we met in someone's home. The scripture we read that night was about Jesus' healing people. We were eager and inquisitive enough to say, "Hey, let's see if He heals us today!"

We needed a body to work on, so we asked if anyone needed a healing. An attractive girl I went to school with spoke up and said that she had always walked with a limp because one leg was about an inch and a half shorter than the other one. We were a little skeptical until she showed us her built up shoe. Then we got excited. This could be a real miracle. We all gathered around her to watch what we were *expecting* to see. Believe me, I didn't close my eyes for that prayer!

As she sat in one chair and stretched her legs out to rest on another, one of the leaders laid his hands on her legs and began to pray. During the prayer I saw her leg grow quickly to the same length as the other leg. She stood up and walked without a limp! The Lord was faithful to follow the teaching of His word with an attesting miracle. We believed in His miracle-working power and He responded with a beautiful, life-changing miracle.

The wonderful little Lutheran church that allowed us to use their facilities would probably have been shocked one night. The leader of our group read some scripture from the book of Acts about the disciples speaking in other languages supernaturally. We thought that was a pretty cool miracle! Being raised in a conservative Baptist church, I had never even heard of those scriptures. We wondered if this was another miracle that could still happen, so we asked God about it and decided to check it out.

With none of us really knowing what to do, we sat in a circle and prayed silently asking God to show us if this was something real that He wanted for us today. All of a sudden I heard the leader shout and start laughing. He very excitedly came around to each of us and said, "Just open your mouth and start talking and see what comes out!" When I did, the strangest sounding stuff came out of my mouth. It sounded like a child's made up play language. This couldn't be the miracle. It sounded too funny!

I tried starting and stopping it. That was easy. I soon realized I could think about something unrelated and still speak this "language." It didn't appear to be coming from my mind at all.

I was still skeptical this funny sounding stream of syllables was the miracle I had questioned. I asked the girl next to me if she could do it yet. When she replied no, I asked her to repeat after me. She could repeat a few syllables, but we quickly realized that without the miracle, she couldn't keep up a steady stream of this newfound language.

I discovered over the months ahead, this miracle was mine to keep. It was a gift from God. I didn't understand at this early age the benefits of this amazing gift. It wasn't until I joined a Spirit-filled church in my late twenties that I began to realize how this gift strengthens your spirit and brings supernatural understanding and revelation at times when we need answers. God's mysteries are so awesome!

As our little group met in the weeks and months to come, we poured over the scriptures and saw many different kinds of miracles and healings take place as we discovered these things were available to us. Our knowledge of God the Father, Jesus, and the Holy Spirit increased dramatically that year.

Then came the time for some of the people to graduate and move and others to lose interest in the "novelty" of our experience. But I would never forget the impressive majesty of our Lord's grace, manifested through our childlike faith as we sought and found. As we knocked, and it was opened unto us.

The most treasured time I've had with the Lord happened the following year. While visiting my aunt and uncle in Tallahassee, I went on a blind date with a nice young man who attended their conservative Episcopal church.

What a date! We went to three different Christian get-togethers of various denominations, but the second place we stopped was extraordinary.

As we stepped into the basement room in the home, I could feel and hear the overwhelming power of the Holy Spirit circulating. The sound was like the quietly powerful hum you hear at a large electrical generating station. The air felt dense with peace and yet somehow light. I could feel the current of energy, which seemed to rotate in a circular motion around the room. I could sense this was no ordinary prayer meeting!

The small room had seats for about twenty around the walls. I noticed the variety of people who were our age to the very old. There were only two seats left on opposite sides of the room, and as a white-haired, kind faced little lady patted the seat next to her, I went to it. As we took our seats, the most unbelievable singing and praising began. I've never experienced anything like it, before or since.

With the powerful hum of the Holy Spirit circulating, we began to sing in unison a melody that I instinctively knew none of us had ever heard before. I have been in wonderful praise and worship services where the harmony was spectacular, but this was different. This wasn't harmony. We were singing exactly the same words and notes as they flowed up out of our spirits. It was as if we were all singing from the same sheet of music. *How is this possible?* I thought.

Then we all began singing in another language unknown to me, yet again, every one of us sang exactly the same words and melody in this beautiful language. At one point I could hear what sounded like a heavenly choir singing, with bells and chimes filling the background. In reverential awe, I thought, *Is that the sound of angels?*

We seemed to float our way to the next Christian get together, and later I wished I had discovered who these people were who knew the Lord so well. Being in the

Lord's presence was exquisite, powerful, and completely unforgettable. So incredible it seemed like a dream.

At this time in my life, the Lord was moving in such supernatural ways on such a frequent basis, I didn't think it would ever come to an end. Much to my sorrow, all of the supernatural experiences ceased for many years as I lost touch with other believers who were seeking and knocking, as I was. I didn't know how to move on with God on my own, and I didn't know where to begin looking for help. I had already traveled into the exciting, supernatural world of God's kingdom and I didn't want to regress into a powerless, lackluster Christian existence. What was I to do? What I did was nothing for many years.

However, I couldn't forget the treasured moments. The Lord had let me taste of His richness with a sip from His supernatural goblet because I sought. He allowed me get a glimpse of His world because I knocked.

As an Adult

Then came what I refer to as "the closet years." I kept Jesus shut in the closet of my heart, and I allowed my strong will to dictate the events of my life over the next ten years.

I periodically looked for a church that had the life and power of the Lord, but to no avail. Being raised a little Baptist girl, I was afraid of what might go on in a "Pentecostal" church. I just knew they were supposed to roll up and down the aisles! And sadly, I couldn't find a denominational church that seemed *alive* with the presence of the Lord like what I experienced with my young prayer group.

I told myself I had to keep Jesus deep inside of me so that no one could trample on that special part of my life. Mistakenly, I thought I was protecting something very delicate. I was actually hiding the greatest man who ever lived just as effectively as putting Him in a hidden room every time I had company.

Fortunately for us, the Lord is faithful and merciful. He doesn't give up on us even when we deserve it.

The Holy Spirit kept nudging me to get involved in a church. At this time I had moved to a different city and I didn't know how to find a church of believers that I was like-minded with and had His life-giving powerful presence.

My uncle Bob was an Episcopal priest during his life, and when he learned I was in search of a Spirit-filled church, he recommended an Episcopal church that was "very radical" at that time for that denomination. They even had a baptistery! (A place to be baptized by total emersion.) That clinched it for me.

As I visited there, I found the *life* I was looking for when we praised and worshiped the Lord. So, for several years (yes, years!) I "visited" the church while the Holy Spirit continued to impress me to get involved. I didn't listen very well, because I was still lord of my life.

When finally the Lord dealt with me regarding the healing of my knee, I discovered my priorities had been in the wrong order. For years I had been afraid to seek

Him, because His holiness and awesome presence were frightening in comparison to the sinful nature I had cultivated. I realized I must make many changes in my life if I was going to be pleasing to God.

It was time to put down roots in this church I was "visiting." I didn't really know how to go about getting involved, so I looked at the list of classes that were offered and decided to take "Park Bench Evangelism" that Russ Moffitt was teaching. It just "so happened" that Russ had served in the navy with my husband's father and had known their family for years!

Under Russ's tutelage we learned to share our testimony, and I became very close to many in the class. This was the springboard that launched me into many areas of service in the church.

After praying for the Lord to guide me to the area He wanted me in, I saw a notice announcing a meeting for concerned parents regarding children's church. While attending this meeting I heard myself say that I would be glad to get involved in this ministry. I couldn't believe the words had come out of my mouth! I had no desire to work with children. The Lord must have known I needed a training ground suitable to my spiritual age!

If you've ever felt like you were supposed to teach but did not feel qualified, I can certainly relate. The amazing and beautiful way of the Lord is to draw us deeper into our relationship with Him by helping us stretch beyond what we feel are our limits.

Teaching helped me to grow. If I wanted to offer my students something fresh from the Lord that would be just what they needed, I had to spend a good deal of time in prayer and in the word. Then I would turn my eyes of faith to Him and trust He would give me the message and guide the lesson.

As I sought the Lord during the years I taught the little children, He impressed upon me, "*Teach them to praise and worship Me.*" Every week He guided me to a different story for them and reminded me to teach them how to praise and worship Him.

As the weeks and months with the children turned into years, I began to see that to really worship the Lord involved coming to Him just like a little child. We have to peel off all the roles and responsibilities we carry around every day and come to Him as a vulnerable, adoring child. Of course He welcomes our prayers and petitions, but first of all He wants to love and be loved the simple way that children do. The "hug" that says I love you just because you're you. After we truly love and worship Him in this way, we can have the real Father/child relationship that He wants and we need.

"And He called a child to Himself and set him before them, and said, '*Truly I say to you, unless you are converted and become like children, you shall not enter the kingdom of heaven*'" (Matthew 18:2–3).

As we come full circle from the adult to "the child" in us, we'll have the proper perspective and relationship we need with our Creator. As a child we trust our heavenly Father. As a child we continue to come before our "Daddy's" throne and spend time sitting at His feet. With the adoring acceptance of a child for its parent, we nestle into our Father's bosom and "hug" Him with arms that will never let go. Because we love Him. Because He is ours.

CHECKLIST

1) Have you found your *church home?*

2) Have you allowed the Holy Spirit to guide you to the area of *service* the Lord would have you in?

3) Have you "*hugged*" your heavenly Father, today?

I cannot encourage you too strongly to get involved in the church the Holy Spirit directs you to. This will be your "battalion." Without a group of like-minded believers to back us up in battle, we can suffer terrible casualties. Without troops to march with, not very much ground will be taken back from the enemy. This doesn't mean attending services whenever it's convenient. This means getting in the trenches with the other soldiers on a regular basis.

We all have a unique and special story to tell of our experiences with the Lord. Some are seemingly more exciting or interesting than our own, but there is someone who needs to hear what the Lord has done in *your* life. It may make a life-changing difference to them.

Won't you tell someone, today?

CHAPTER 5

THE HEARING EAR

Have you ever been determined to hear from God and been disappointed? I think there are a lot of people who have tried at one time or another to reach out to God for an answer or direction and didn't quite make the connection. Maybe that's why most people I talk to don't believe they can hear from Him.

Jesus said, *"My sheep hear My voice,* and I know them, and they follow Me" (John 10:27). And also, "Behold, I stand at the door and knock; *if anyone hears My voice and opens the door, I will come in to him,* and will dine with him, and he with Me" (Rev. 3:20).

Jesus said His followers would hear His voice. Could it be He's speaking and the sheep (that's us!) haven't learned to recognize their Master's voice?

I believe He is trying to communicate with us frequently and in different ways, but we are oblivious to it due to interference in the path of communication.

You know what it sounds like when you're on the phone and there is a lot of static or interference in the line? You can't hear what the person on the other end is saying. If it's bad enough, you can't even tell who is calling.

When we were in the electronics business, I learned interference is referred to as "static" or "noise." You get static when impurities enter or touch the line of communication. We had people call us all the time and tell us something was wrong with their TV because they had static on their screen. We had to educate them that static is caused by inadequate reception...not the TV itself. The antenna or cable or satellite—whatever was being used to "pick up" the signal—was the problem. There was a breakdown in the communication process, rather than something being wrong with the sender (the TV station) or receiver (the TV).

When we don't hear from God, there is interference in our lines of communication with Him. Nothing is wrong with Him (who is sending messages) or us (who the messages are being sent to), but rather in our *process* of hearing from Him.

In this chapter we'll try to uncover the mysteries of the communication process. We'll look at what we can do to remove impurities from our lines of communication, improve reception, and ultimately hear our Leader's voice.

Part I—Our Preparation

We all want instant answers. I'm sure the Lord would like instant responses from us as well! The truth of the matter is it takes time to develop our lines of communication with the Lord. And the more prepared we are, the quicker and easier it is to hear from Him.

I've discovered five ingredients that really help to develop clear lines of communication with our Lord and King. They take some time to develop but are invaluable in our quest to hear from God.

1. *Bow Down—Holy Lifestyle*

When people come into the presence of a king, it is customary to bow or kneel. This act of *obeisance* shows a deep respect or reverence and denotes the king's lordship.

Psalm 95:6–7a says, "Come, let us worship and *bow down*; let us *kneel* before the Lord our Maker. For He is our God, and we are the people of His pasture and the sheep of His hand."

In Hebrew, *kara* is the word used in this verse for "bow," meaning to bend the knee; by impl. to sink, to prostrate: bow (down, self), bring down (low).[6]

Anyone can make an outward show of homage to a king. The real proof of their allegiance comes through their *lifestyle*. A loyal subject will lay down their very life for their king.

As loyal subjects of Christ the King, *we choose to make ourselves lower as we place His Lordship over us.* This is in effect "bending our knee" to Him. As we lower ourselves before Him, we make ourselves subject to *His desires, first.*

Oops! That doesn't sound like very much fun, does

it? Those of us living in a democratic society, at the very least, expect to have our desires consulted and considered. And if we win, we get our way!

Our heavenly Father already knows our desires and wants what is best for our overall development. If we're willing to trust that He's smarter and has a better plan than we could ever hope to dream of, then our lifestyle should reflect *obedience* to His commands.

First, we need to be obedient to the simple things He's outlined in His word. To love, share, give cheerfully, take care of the downtrodden, forgive, be fair and honest, temperate, honor those in authority over us, and be thankful in all things and above all to reverence God. Then comes obedience to His plan for our lives.

Through an *obedient and subjected lifestyle,* we will gain blessings, honor, and clear reception from our Lord.

2. *Pleasing Attitude—Praise*

Here's an easy one…praise clears the air!

"I will *give thanks* to the Lord with all my heart; I will *tell of all Thy wonders.* I will *be glad* and *exult* in Thee; I will *sing praise* to Thy name, O Most High" (Psalm 9:1–2).

Praise on our lips is an indication of what is in our heart. When we are full of self, we don't feel like praising very much. When we are full of the Lord, we feel like praising all of the time. Jesus said, "…out of the abundance of the heart the mouth speaketh" (Matthew 12:34b, KJV).

Praise is an interesting phenomenon. It not only flows

out of our spirit when we are full of the Lord, but also helps *refill* us when we run dry. Sort of like the pump in a re-circulating fountain. When the pump gets turned off, no fountain. But all you have to do to turn the fountain back on is start the pump again. Praise!

Here's a wild idea to think about. I was working on this section and went to the kitchen to get a glass of water. In mid-stride this sentence jumped into my thoughts... *Praise attracts positive telekinetic energy.* I stopped in my tracks and skeptically said, "What?! Isn't telekinesis when people try to move objects with the force of their mind?" I decided to look it up and pray about it to determine if this was a God inspired idea.

What I found out was, (1) *kinetic* means "of or having to do with motion."[7] *Tele* means "having to go with operating over long distances."[8] (2) *Energy* is *positive* because *it is real and present.* (Example: light is a positive thing; darkness is only the absence of light.)[9]

Putting this all together, I deducted that as we praise, real and present action or energy occurs over long distances. So, if we want to make things happen...praise!

The opposite of praise is murmuring and complaining. What do you suppose that it attracts?

Today, if you would *hear His voice,* do not harden your hearts, as at *Meribah,* as in the day of *Massah* in the wilderness;

"*When your fathers tested Me, they tried Me, though they had seen My work. For forty years I loathed that generation, and said they are a people who err in their*

heart, and do not know My ways. Therefore I swore in My anger, truly they shall not enter into My rest."
Psalm 95:7b-11

Massah and *Meribah* (meaning testing and strife) was the place where the Israelites didn't trust God to provide water for them in the wilderness. They grumbled, complained, and quarreled with Moses because they were thirsty. They tested the Lord, saying, "Is the Lord among us, or not?" (Exodus 17:7).

When we grumble and complain, we're really saying, "I don't like my circumstances, and I don't trust God to take care of me." Complaining is the opposite of faith.

As we can see in the case of the Israelites, they irritated our heavenly Father for forty years! So much so He swore they would never enter His rest.

I used to complain about things people did that I didn't like, all the time to whoever would listen. One particular person that I was around a lot was especially hard for me to deal with. In my frustration of not knowing how to deal with them, I would call and discuss my problems with friends or family members—one after another. It seemed that no matter how I prayed or what I did, the problems remained.

One day I was praying and asking the Lord to show me why I was "going around the same mountain" again and again with this person. Immediately, the word "*backbiting*" leaped out at me. I was stunned. But as I thought about it, I realized I was confessing my problems. I was talking about people behind their backs and was murmuring and complaining like the Israelites did.

From that moment on, I vowed to quit complaining and start thanking the Lord for all my blessings. And eventually those things I once complained about happened less and less.

Next time our mouths open to complain about something, let's remember the Israelites and praise instead!

Finally, *praise changes our hearts, our inner being*. I picture our hearts before praising, like a creeping caterpillar. Slow, ugly, vulnerable, able to sting people, and living to satisfy its voracious appetite. When we praise, our hearts go through a metamorphosis like a caterpillar in its cocoon. Our inner self is transformed into something beautiful, like a butterfly.

"Praise the Lord, for the Lord is good; sing praises to His name, for it is *lovely*" (Psalm 135:3).

Like the life span of the butterfly, our heart change is short-lived so we need to keep on praising throughout the day!

"Through Him then, let us *continually* offer up a sacrifice of praise to God, that is, the fruit of lips that give thanks to His name" (Hebrews 13:15).

As we *clear the air with praise* for our heavenly King, He responds with His presence, favor and joy.

3. *Steadfast Worship*

Steadfast is a word you don't hear much anymore!

> My heart is *steadfast*, O God; I will sing, I will sing praises, even with my soul. Awake, harp and lyre; I will awaken the dawn! I will give thanks to Thee, O LORD, among the peoples; and I will sing praises to Thee among the nations, for Thy lovingkindness is great above the heavens; and Thy truth reaches to the skies. Be exalted, O God, above the heavens, and Thy glory above all the earth. Psalm 108:1–5

Steadfast means *loyal; unwavering; not changing; firm of purpose.*[10] No wonder it's going out of style! Our society doesn't regard loyalty and firm purpose as highly as it used to. We've been let down by the immorality of many leaders and the broken promises of those we've trusted.

No worries with the Lord our King! In Him we can steadfastly trust. In Him we *must* steadfastly trust. Out of that unwavering trust comes an intense love and adoration for our Creator. That expressed is *worship*.

Worship differs from praise somewhat. Praise extols the virtues and accomplishments. Worship loves, admires, and adores. Both praise and worship are expressions of appreciation, but praise without worship is incomplete.

When my children thank me for something I've done, I'm glad they are grateful and appreciative. But when they cuddle up next to me and say, "Mom, I love you," it melts my heart.

Our heavenly Father, Jesus, and the Holy Spirit have feelings and emotions. Remember, one of Jehovah's names is Qanna or Jealous (Exodus 34:14). He is jealous of our love and attention to others when it is greater than to Him. He wants to hear how much we love Him, just like we need to have love expressed to us.

Worship is more than a simple "I love you," though. *It is placing something or someone in an exalted position in our lives.*

My previous pastor, Charles B. Fulton, Jr., challenged us in one of his sermons to take a reality check. What consumes most of our thinking? Work, food, sex, play, things, people, places...or God? What do we do with our time? Our actions speak even louder to our Lord than our words. Does He take an exalted place in our thoughts, actions, and time; or does He come in second, third, or even last place?

As soldiers in the Lord's army, we make as part of our ongoing training, the discipline of a worshipful lifestyle. I say discipline because it's not part of our natural instincts to put something or someone above our own needs or wants. But, when we make a conscious decision to *steadfastly keep the Lord as our primary focus, adoring Him with all of our heart, our "antenna" will be raised to catch the "signal" that He is sending.* And oh, that is so worth it! He is so worth it!

Exalt the LORD our God, and *worship* at His footstool; holy is He.
Moses and Aaron were among His priests, and

Samuel was among those who called on His name;
they called upon the LORD, and He answered them.
Psalm 99:5–6

4. *Glorify His Name*

When I was young, I didn't understand the ways of the Lord. I heard some people exclaim, "Glory!" when they got excited about something good in their lives. I thought it was pretty funny. When we *glorify* something or someone, it's not funny. *We give them great honor and respect.*

Psalm 22:23 tells us, "You who fear the Lord, praise Him; all you descendants of Jacob, *glorify* Him, and stand in awe of Him, all you descendants of Israel."

You've probably heard of the World War II fighter pilots called *kamikaze* or *divine wind.* These pilots volunteered for suicide missions in which they purposely flew their planes full of explosives into enemy targets. The kamikazes are remembered for their loyalty, dedication, and bravery as they willingly gave their lives for their emperor.

The kamikazes considered it a privilege to glorify their leader with their highest respect and honor. Soldiers in the U.S. Armed Forces are taught it is a privilege to die for our country and the principles it was founded on.

To what degree are we as soldiers in the Lord's army, willing to glorify our heavenly King? Are we willing to *surrender our lives in dedication?*

Or do you not know that your body is a temple

of the Holy Spirit who is in you, whom you have from God, and that *you are not your own? For you have been bought with a price:* therefore *glorify God in your body.* 1 Corinthians 6:19–20

In some cultures, when you save a person's life, they in return dedicate their life to you out of thanksgiving and appreciation. They become a *bond-slave* or one who gives/sells their life for a debt too large to repay.

When we chose Jesus to be our Lord and Savior, we accepted the ransom price of His life in exchange for ours. He didn't "purchase" us with the intention that we'd go off and leave Him! No, He saved us so we could be adopted relatives—not strangers.

Let's take this a step further. If we've been *bought* with the price of Jesus' own blood and we belong to Him and not ourselves, then shouldn't we be living to glorify Him—*instead of living to make ourselves happy?*

I found out happiness can be an idol. Listening to the thought-provoking messages on "The Inner Life" tape series by Joyce Meyer, I realized happiness was an idol in my life. Achieving happiness was of paramount importance to me. Happiness meant having health, prosperity, and especially harmony in my home. Most of my thoughts and prayers focused on achieving happiness for others and myself.

When I peacefully accepted that glorifying God should come even before my individual happiness, I surrendered myself to the Lord prayerfully, in order to glorify Him. Then I was pleasantly surprised to find my soul able to relax. I felt relief in not striving to achieve an idyllic life all the time. Hurts became less important, and doing what the Lord called me to do became of utmost importance.

When we glorify Him, He in turn brings His peace and joy beyond description. As we *dedicate our lives to the glory of His name, then all the other things we need will be given to us.* Including clear reception!

> Teach me Thy way, O LORD; I will walk in Thy truth; unite my heart to fear Thy name. I will give thanks to Thee, O LORD my God, with all my heart, and will *glorify Thy name forever.* Psalm 86:11–12

5. *Wait on His Presence with Diligence*

Waiting on the Lord is a little like planning a birthday party for someone. You invite the guest of honor and *expect* them to show up. When they arrive, the party begins!

"Lead me in Thy truth and teach me, for Thou art the God of my salvation; *for Thee I wait all the day*" (Psalm 25:5). Can you wait "all the day"? That's a tough one, isn't it?

When the Lord's manifest or evident presence is with us, it's as wonderful as any party could be, so why do we have so much difficulty waiting on the guest of honor?

1) *Waiting requires faith.* The Hebrew word for wait (used in Psalm 25:5) is *qavah,* which figuratively means to *expect:* gather (together), look, patiently, tarry, wait (for, on, upon).[11] To *expect* requires faith that what

we are anticipating will occur. Faith clears the air spiritually. Remember, faith is our shield, which will quench all the fiery darts of the enemy. *Our trust and belief in the presence of the Lord in our lives, opens up "the airways."*

"And *without faith it is impossible to please Him,* for he who comes to God *must believe that He is, and that He is a rewarder* of those who seek Him" (Hebrews 11:6).

2) *Waiting requires patience.* In today's instant society, patience for any length of time is becoming a rare and unusual thing. We want it now!

Up until this century, people had to wait for almost everything. Transportation, farming, industry, and homemaking were time consuming and labor intensive. Waiting was part of their lifestyle.

Today, waiting is almost a lost skill. We need to develop it in our lifestyle as we learn to wait on the Lord. And as with any learned skill, it requires *practice, work,* and *discipline.*

To *practice* means you have to do it again and again. We never get great at anything unless we do it!

To *work* at patiently waiting requires that we put forth some effort to do something that's not always easy to do. Anything and everything seems to come up when we try to wait on the Lord. Distractions and interruptions reach new heights. But persevere! His felt presence is more than worth it.

And finally, to *discipline* ourselves to consistently wait on His presence is our ultimate goal. As we every day, all through the day, seek Him expectantly in all things, He responds with answers, signs, and the wonderful peace and joy of His presence!

"Yet those who *wait for the Lord* will gain new strength; they will mount up with wings like eagles, they will run and not get tired, they will walk and not become weary" (Isaiah 40:31).

Part II—The Lord Speaks

When we accept Jesus as our Savior, He gives us a fabulous gift...

> And Peter said to them, "Repent, and let each of you be baptized in the name of Jesus Christ for the forgiveness of your sins; and you shall *receive the gift of the Holy Spirit.* For the promise is for you and your children, and for all who are far off, as many as the LORD our God shall call to Himself." Acts 2:38–39

Our heavenly Father knew we would need a Helper to enable us to stay in contact with Him. The Holy Spirit is our supply line and means of communication to our Commander-in-Chief. As He lives in us—guiding, teaching, encouraging, comforting and helping us—He equips us to be *"receivers"* of the Lord.

> [Jesus said,] "But when He, the Spirit of truth, comes, He will guide you into all the truth; *for He will not speak on His own initiative, but whatever*

He hears, He will speak; and He will disclose to you what is to come." John 16:13

Our Helper discloses to us the truth of God, so we can be *"transmitters"* to those people He places in our paths.

> For *to us God revealed them through the Spirit; for the Spirit searches all things, even the depths* of God. For who among men knows the thoughts of a man except the spirit of the man, which is in him? Even so the thoughts of God no one knows except the Spirit of God.
>
> Now we have received, not the spirit of the world, but the Spirit who is from God, that we might know the things freely given to us by God, which things we also speak, *not in words taught by human wisdom, but in those taught by the Spirit, combining spiritual thoughts with spiritual words.* 1 Corinthians 2:10–13

The Spirit of God speaks to us in many ways. In this section we'll examine the obvious and not so obvious ways our precious Communicator reveals truth to us.

His Word

The voice of God is always present in His word, but do we hear it? Do we read the word primarily for guidelines for godly living, or with the intention of hearing a *personal message* spoken directly to us?

How is it possible to receive a personal message? First,

it helps to ask Him for it! James 4:2 says we don't have because we don't ask God.

When the Lord speaks to us through His word, the scriptures will evoke a "Yes!" response from our spirit. He may give us a message during Bible study. Other times He might bring a particular book, chapter, or verse of the Bible to mind. Our job is to read it, study it, and pray about it until He gives us the understanding from it.

One evening I was seeking the Lord about what He wanted me to do in our church. As I knelt next to my bed and began intently praying—asking what area of service He would like me in, all of a sudden the words "Isaiah 58" appeared imprinted in my mind like a typewritten phrase.

Curiously, I got up and pulled out my Bible to see what Isaiah 58 said. It began, "Cry loudly, do not hold back; raise your voice like a trumpet, and declare to My people...." As I read the rest of the chapter, my heart pounded and I was filled with dread because I knew the Lord was telling me to read this to our church congregation. This was no pat on the back, "You're doing a great job" message. It was a stern word, and I didn't want to deliver it!

The Lord kept bringing this chapter to my mind over the next two weeks, so I decided I'd call our pastor and ask him if he would allow me to read it. Unfortunately, I wasn't able to get in touch with him and Sunday rolled around.

My heart felt like it was going to beat out of my chest all that Sunday morning. I went to church and the words in the praise music said, "I heard you calling in the night...here I am Lord...send me." It completely confirmed my worst fear—I had to give the message.

When the praise and worship time ended, it felt as if someone's hand propelled me forward to the front of the church. I read Isaiah 58 with, what sounded like to my ears, a supernaturally booming voice. Then immediately left with the children to teach children's church.

Later that morning, several people stopped me and said, "Good word." I was puzzled until the youth pastor asked if I knew in advance that the pastor was going to preach on Isaiah 58 that Sunday. I was floored! I ran to see Fr. Charles to confirm the story. He not only confirmed it, but said he could have been knocked off the platform with a feather when I began reading the same scripture that He was going to preach about!

Isn't the Lord amazing?! He certainly is full of surprises! If we will only try to recognize what He is saying to us through His word, we will discover the thrill of His personal message to us.

A Still Small Voice

In this day and age, if you tell people that you hear "voices," they'll think you belong in a mental ward!

We have risen to such heights intellectually, that we as a society no longer believe anything we can't explain. We congratulate ourselves that we are no longer pagan and uncivilized, yet we've lost some ancient truths along the way that were at one time common knowledge.

Presently, things of the spirit world and supernatural

occurrences are relegated to TV shows, curiosity seekers, devil-worshipers, and God-seekers. Not exactly mainstream America!

Since we're God-seekers and different from the norm, we open ourselves up for ridicule and rejection when we state our belief in the less talked about realities in God's word. However, unless we boldly trust in God's whole word, it cannot make the impact it should in our lives.

With all of that said, let's embrace the fact that the sovereign God of the universe wants to have a one on one relationship with each one of us. If He created the worlds, don't you think He has the capability to speak to each one of us individually? Do you think He created us as some sort of science project—or because He loves us? And if He loves us so much that He gave His only begotten Son to die for us, don't you think He wants to communicate with the objects of His love?

What do you suppose the Lord's *voice* sounds like? It is described in 1 Kings 19:12 (KJV), as "*a still small voice.*"

> And he said, "Go forth, and stand upon the mount before the LORD." And behold, the LORD passed by, and a great and strong wind rent the mountains, and brake in pieces the rocks before the LORD; but the LORD was not in the wind: and after the wind an earthquake; but the LORD was not in the earthquake: and after the earthquake a fire; but the LORD was not in the fire: and after the fire *a still small voice.*
>
> And it was so, when Elijah heard it, that he

wrapped his face in his mantle, and went out, and stood in the entering in of the cave. And behold, *there came a voice unto him,* and said, "What doest thou here, Elijah?" 1 Kings 19:11–13 (KJV)

Elijah was a man of God, and he recognized the Lord's voice and was not afraid to acknowledge it. If we are people of God, then we should be open and receptive to the "still small voice" of the Lord.

I heard the wife of a famous preacher say the reason the Lord's voice is a "still small voice" is because you have to get *real* close to hear it!

Once when I was seeking the Lord for direction, that still small voice seemed to shout at me! Just before my grandmother went to be with the Lord, she gave me a very special hand-made bracelet that she had picked up in her travels and that I had admired all my life.

This Incan silver bracelet was intricately handcrafted with fascinating little three dimensional figures. I was thrilled with the gift, but before I had a chance to wear it, my oldest daughter said, "Mom, I think you ought to pray about it before you wear that bracelet."

I didn't want to pray about it; I wanted to wear it! So I did, but the Holy Spirit put a check in my spirit that something wasn't right.

I decided to visit the library and see what I could find in Incan literature about the funny little characters that were designed into my bracelet. Much to my dismay, I discovered these characters were ancient Incan gods! Sadly, I decided to put the bracelet up.

A week went by and I began to rationalize to myself that just because the figures were gods of the Incas, they weren't *my* gods. I decided that it couldn't possibly hurt to just wear the bracelet. After all, *I* wasn't worshiping those gods! So I put the bracelet back on.

Along came my daughter Heather and, seeing the bracelet on my arm, said, "I really think you ought to pray before you wear that." I knew in my heart she was right, but I didn't want to pray about it because I was afraid of what the answer might be.

The next day I received a letter from our church, asking us to prayerfully consider a financial gift toward the replacement of a badly needed roof. I decided to take this and the bracelet question to the Lord for guidance.

I sat at the kitchen table and purposely placed the bracelet on top of the letter. I folded my arms and leaned over, resting my forehead on my arms. In that second, I heard a very loud voice in my spirit commanding, "*Remove the abomination from the holy letter!*" My eyes flew open wide with astonishment, I lifted my head slowly, and said, "Uh oh. Things aren't looking too good for the bracelet!"

I continued to earnestly seek the Lord for another thirty minutes, and finally He spoke these words to me in a *still small voice*, "*The trinket is not a fitting adornment for my temple.*" As I sadly pondered these words, I realized He was telling me my body was His temple and placing little foreign gods as a decoration on His temple was unacceptable. Crestfallen, I resigned myself to not wear the bracelet.

I then asked what amount of money to give toward the

new church roof, and He replied again in that *still small voice, "Sacrifice the trinket, for it will be a true sacrifice."* Oh, how right He was!

In this example the Lord's voice was first as loud as a shout, then later, very still and quiet. *He used words that I would not normally use,* such as "trinket" and "adornment" and referring to my body as His "temple." *He gave me direction that I didn't want to hear, but knew in my heart was correct. The direction was scriptural.* All of these together confirmed it was the voice of God, not my mind or the enemy "playing tricks" on me.

It can be very hard to distinguish between the voice of God, our own mind, and the deceiver. *We must be very careful* about following the direction of voices. Ask the Lord for confirmation, and if it's Him leading you, He'll confirm His word another way. And we can be certain that if the direction doesn't line up with the word of God, it isn't from God.

Hearing the Lord's voice and having it confirmed, is one of the most exciting things that can happen in our Christian walk. Don't be afraid of it, reject it, or even the opposite, seek it exclusively. I have only heard Him speak this way a handful of times in my life. It is not the norm for most of us, but it is a powerful, wonderful, unforgettable experience.

As we seek the Lord and His kingdom, He will communicate to us in many different ways, each one as precious and special as He is!

Dreams and Visions

Sometimes the Lord uses more dramatic ways of communicating to us. In *dreams and visions,* the Lord supernaturally *shows* us things of importance.

> ...and behold, the glory of the God of Israel was coming from the way of the east. And *His voice* was like the sound of many waters; and the earth shone with His glory. And it was like *the appearance of the vision which I saw,* like the vision which I saw when He came to destroy the city. And the visions were like the vision which I saw by the river Chebar; and I fell on my face.
>
> And the glory of the LORD came into the house by the way of the gate facing toward the east. And the Spirit lifted me up and brought me into the inner court; and behold, the glory of the LORD filled the house.
>
> Then I heard one speaking to me from the house, while a man was standing beside me. And He said to me, "Son of man, this is the place of My throne and the place of the soles of My feet, where I will dwell among the sons of Israel forever. And the house of Israel will not again defile My holy name..." Ezekiel 43:2–7a

Ezekiel describes his incredible vision when the Lord came to give him instructions for His sanctuary. The voice he heard was like "the sound of many waters." What he saw was overwhelmingly impressive and awesome.

The Lord showed Ezekiel His greatness in preparation for the orders He was mandating. The Lord knew what Ezekiel needed to see for him to understand the importance of carrying out the necessary instructions.

I was in the spirit on the Lord's day, and *I heard behind me a voice like the sound of a trumpet,* saying, "Write in a book what you see, and send it to the seven churches: to Ephesus and to Smyrna and to Pergamum and to Thyatira and to Sardis and to Philadelphia and to Laodicea."

And I turned *to see the voice that was speaking with me.* And having turned I saw seven golden lampstands; and in the middle of the lampstands one like a son of man, clothed in a robe reaching to the feet, and girded across His breast with a golden girdle. And His head and His hair were white like white wool, like snow; and His eyes were like a flame of fire; and His feet were like burnished bronze, when it has been caused to glow in a furnace, and *His voice was like the sound of many waters.* And in His right hand He held seven stars; and out of His mouth came a sharp two-edged sword; and His face was like the sun shining in its strength.

And when I saw Him, I fell at His feet as a dead man. And He *laid His right hand upon me,* saying, "Do not be afraid; I am the first and the last, and the living One; and I was dead, and behold, I am alive forevermore, and I have the keys of death and of Hades.

"Write therefore the things which you have seen, and the things which are, and the things which shall take place after these things." Revelation 1:10–19

John was given a pictorial revelation for the purpose of preparing the bondservants of Christ for the enormity of what was to come. In this revelation, he *saw, heard, and was touched by the Lord.*

> And it came about that as he journeyed, he was approaching Damascus, and suddenly a *light from heaven flashed around him;* and he fell to the ground, *and heard a voice* saying to him, "Saul, Saul, why are you persecuting Me?"
> And he said, "Who art Thou, LORD?" And He said, "I am Jesus whom you are persecuting, but rise, and enter the city, and it shall be told you what you must do." And *the men who traveled with him stood speechless, hearing the voice, but seeing no one.* Acts 9:3–7

Saul, also known as Paul, heard the audible voice of Jesus accompanied by blinding light. The men with him also heard Jesus' voice, but saw "no one." Visions can be seen, heard, felt, and *experienced by more than one person.* These spectacular kinds of visions are "open-eyed."

The less spectacular but more common types of visions are seen "close-eyed." *The Spirit may give special dreams to us,* or He may reveal something to us by *placing a "picture" in our mind.* These are the ones that are easy to miss.

The "pictures" the Lord gives us may seem at first like our own imagination, but (1) *they don't go away easily,* (2) *they tend to be unusual,* and (3) *our spirit witnesses to it.* The pictures I see always come during prayer.

When I'm praying with someone, sometimes I'll get a mental image of something that is seemingly unrelated to what we are praying about. I've found that if I stop praying and ask God to explain what He's trying to *illustrate* to me, the results are astounding!

When I was praying with a friend one time I saw a picture of hands hanging on to a lone branch protruding from the face of a cliff. When we stopped and asked the Lord for the meaning, all of a sudden I understood that it represented her daughter's hands clenching tightly onto her troubled marriage. The Lord wanted her to let go and trust Him for His ultimate purpose.

When my friend shared with her daughter what I had seen, *it confirmed* to her what the Spirit had impressed her to do. *Spiritual visions and dreams should be confirmed, before being acted upon!* Not only do we have active imaginations, but the enemy's job is to mislead and deceive us.

Some practical tips here: I have found in my experience, that normally the logical conclusion I might draw from a "picture" is not usually the message the Lord is trying to relay. Only after seeking Him to reveal His meaning—and then waiting until the next part unveils—does His true revelation unfold. Many times there are subsequent pictures that define and make clear the meaning of the revelation. Just stay focused on the Lord and open. Don't rush. And praying in the Spirit seems to clear the channel for better reception, as well.

A word to the wise…if you start seeking visions and dreams, the enemy might just oblige you! Just seek the Lord and when He wants you to see things that illustrate His purpose, be open to recognize them!

Prophets, Teachers, and Preachers of the Word

The Lord has called many to be prophets, teachers, and preachers of His word. Is He calling you?

> Now the word of the LORD came to me saying, "Before I formed you in the womb I knew you, and before you were born I consecrated you; *I have appointed you a prophet* to the nations."
>
> Then I said, "Alas, LORD God! Behold, I do not know how to speak, because I am a youth."
>
> But the LORD said to me, "Do not say, 'I am a youth,' because everywhere I send you, you shall go, and all that I command you, you shall speak. Do not be afraid of them, for I am with you to deliver you," declares the LORD. Then the LORD stretched out His hand and touched my mouth, and the LORD said to me, *"Behold, I have put My words in your mouth."* Jeremiah 1:4–9

As He did in the case of Jeremiah, the Lord chooses to put His words in the mouths of *prophets*. Why? Because (1) *not everyone will seek Him on their own and patiently listen for His voice,* and (2) *He uses a voice to create through the power of His spoken word.*

What is a prophet? *The New Unger's Bible Dictionary* says a prophet is, *"one who is divinely inspired to communicate God's will to His people and to disclose the future to them."* The Hebrew words for "prophet" translate: *to announce, call a declarer, announcer* and also *one who sees* or *seer.*[12] A prophet receives information from God and then delivers it to the addressee.

> But know this first of all, that no prophecy of Scripture is a matter of one's own interpretation, for *no prophecy was ever made by an act of human will, but men moved by the Holy Spirit spoke from God.* 2 Peter 1:20–21

A true prophet of God will "see" or "hear" a message from Him and then will deliver it *at the proper time and place.* A true prophet will *make sure the message is from God.* And a true prophet *delivers words of exhortation and encouragement.* A stern warning without a word of encouragement is uncharacteristic of our Lord.

The messages that a prophet hears are *new messages* (always in line with His word) from the Lord. Teachers and preachers of the word of God take messages that *have already been given* through prophets, and *help us understand them and apply them to our lives.*

I'm not saying that preachers and teachers give old messages! As we study scripture, our Helper will illuminate us with fresh meaning from old verses. Then we take the fresh concept to those He entrusts into our care.

You might say, as I did at first, "Who, me?!" We all come under the category of teacher at some time or another. Jesus told us in Mark 16:15, to "Go into all the world and preach the gospel to all creation." We each have our own portion of the world to speak the good news to, and what we say better be pertinent and timely to their lives or they will not listen.

There is no shortcut when it comes to delivering messages from God. First, we have to receive the message before we can deliver it. How? By becoming good listeners.

My children are great students, but when they brought home their achievement scores every year, the lowest marks were always in listening skills. This was an area that had to be developed.

To really listen, we truly care to hear what's being said. When we truly care about someone, we listen with interest to what they have to say.

The people I consider my friends are ones who care enough about me to ask what's going on in my life and then really listen and respond. I don't necessarily want to talk very much about myself, but I want them to care enough about me that they want to listen.

Our Lord wants us to become good listeners. First to Him, and then to others. He and others *observe our level of interest in them by our degree of listening.*

When we become good listeners, we can carry new

and "re-newed" messages to those the Lord impresses us to. Messages that are pertinent, timely, and important.

Everyday Encounters

Are everyday encounters just chance?

> For since the creation of the world His invisible attributes, His eternal power and divine nature, have been clearly seen, *being understood through what has been made,* so that they are without excuse. Romans 1:20

I think there is a lesson to be learned from everything God has created. Our creator knows we need visual aids to help us understand how things work. He made us with a "show me" mentality. When we became a new creature through Christ Jesus (2 Corinthians 5:17), He gave us new "eyes." When we ask Him to help us see what He wants us to see, ordinary things take on new meaning.

A person I am close to is occasionally critical and hard to get along with. I resented this, until one day I asked the Lord to help me see this person with His eyes. I didn't hear words from heaven or have a supernatural vision. What I did have was an immediate tenderness accompanied by a "knowing" in my spirit, that this person carried deep roots of pain from the past. My anger was replaced by compassion and love. I was seeing with Jesus' eyes.

He also gives us new "ears" to hear spiritually. Everyday occurrences take on new meaning when we're expecting the Lord to speak to us through them. A person who is rude to us may be the Lord saying, "Have patience and forgive them. Bless those who persecute you." An ambulance roaring by may be a prompt to pray for those involved. A friend's advice may be the Lord's skillful and Godly wisdom imparted to us through a chosen vessel. A cut flower, however beautiful may show us that when we are cut off from Him, we soon die spiritually.

The Lord is speaking to us all the time. When we learn to ask in every circumstance, "Lord, what are you trying to tell me in this?" He will open up *everyday encounters* to show us His purpose, love, concern, and voice.

Are we listening?

Part III—Our Response

The key to hearing from God is being a yielded vessel. When we surrender the lordship of our lives to Him, He has the opportunity to give us His perfect guidance. From our glad willingness to submit to His authority comes an ability to hear beyond our own wants and desires. We move into *His* realm.

When we moment by moment relish our relationship with Him, like a little child clinging instinctively to their protective parent, we'll hear Him. As we share our lives with Him and expect Him to share His divine life in return, we'll hear Him. As we listen for His voice in all things, He will make Himself known to us.

Why? Because He *loves* us…"For *God so loved the world, that He gave His only begotten Son,* that whoever believes in Him should not perish, but have eternal life" (John 3:16).

Our heavenly Father created us out of His love. He sent the Word, who became Jesus our Savior, because of His love.

He speaks to us now because He wants what is best for our spirit and the spirits of others. He speaks, hoping we'll care enough to listen.

When we hear the voice of Almighty God, however it may come, it should change our lives. The voice that created worlds will *renew* and *strengthen* us. It will *enable* us to fulfill His divine purpose. And it will *inspire* us to reach out to others.

Before the Bible became so readily available, people relied on their personal relationship with the Lord for guidance, and got it! Did you know Christopher Columbus stated in his journal that it was the Holy Spirit that told him to set sail and find another route to the East Indies?

Now, with God's word in such abundant supply, we don't have to wait on His presence to receive His guidance. He likes us to, but we don't have to. We can go straight to His holy ordinances and receive all the instruction we need. The only problem is then we usually miss the fullness of His wonderful felt presence.

If we don't hear from God, either through His word or otherwise, our spirit starts drying up like a plant that needs water. A communicating relationship with our heavenly Family brings *life* in our spirits. Without God's infusion, we have no spiritual life. Jesus said, "It is written,

'Man shall not live on bread alone, but on every word that proceeds out of the mouth of God'" (Matthew 4:4).

When we truly "hear" a message from the Lord, it comes with confidence, purpose, and inner peace as "witnesses." Be sure to test what you think you are "receiving" to see if it lines up and points to God as the sender.

If you're not sure, keep seeking the Lord until you have one or more of his "witnesses." Be persistent and take the time. If you think the Lord is trying to tell you something, stop what you are doing and seek Him until you get further direction or the impression goes away.

I'll tell you about a time when I didn't stop to seek the Lord…

One morning I was quickly blow-drying my hair in the bathroom and thinking about what I had to do that day. I was supposed to travel to a nearby town and help a salesman show some products I represented to one of his customers.

All of a sudden a little thought ran through my mind, interrupting my thoughts about work. *Cancel your travel plans.* I was startled and immediately asked the Lord if the message was from Him. No answer.

I had mixed emotions. My mind was racing…If I called and cancelled at the last minute, I would look unprofessional. What would be my excuse? I couldn't lie. I didn't have time to stop and seek the Lord 'til I heard Him. I would be late. What should I do?

I hastily said, "Lord, I can't tell if this is from you or

not. If it is, will you please have the salesman I'm supposed to work with call and cancel?" No answer.

So, I drove to the nearby city, worked with the salesman a short time, and stopped at a red light. All of a sudden *bam!* As I started to turn my head to see what happened, tiny bits of flying glass stung the side of my face. I froze for a split second and then my head snapped back at an awkward angle. As I shakily got out and walked around to survey the damage in a daze, I had the sickening realization that I had not responded to the message from the Lord the right way. The whole rear of my very solid Jeep was caved in.

As a result of this accident, I struggled through years of agonizing neck and back pain and memory loss. The Lord is continuing to heal me, but it has been a very, very slow recovery. This could have been prevented if I had *stopped to seek the Lord until I knew what I was supposed to do.*

I don't advocate jumping into something when a message hasn't been confirmed though. That can be just as bad, if it isn't from the Lord. Wait until we know that we know what God wants us to do, and when He wants us to do it. Then we can stay out of "accidents" and hopefully help and encourage others as well.

CHECKLIST

1) Have you chosen to *lower yourself* as you *place His Lordship above you?* Are you gaining clear reception by developing an *obedient* and *subjected* lifestyle?

2) Are you clearing the air with *praise?* Have you *put away murmuring* and *complaining?*

3) Are you "raising your antenna" with *steadfast worship?* Does your *lifestyle* reflect it?

4) To what degree are you willing to *surrender your life* to *glorify His name?*

5) Are you *waiting on the Lord* with *faith* and *patience?* Are you *disciplining* yourself to *consistently wait* on His presence?

6) Have you begun to recognize the *personal messages* given to you through the word?

7) Are you listening for the *still small voice* of the Lord?

8) Are you *seeking the Lord?* Are you receptive to *dreams* and *visions* that illustrate His purpose?

9) Is the Lord calling you to *preach, teach,* or *prophesy* to your corner of the world? Are you *listening for His message, testing,* and *delivering* it?

10) With your new "eyes" and "ears" are you recognizing our Master's voice through *everyday encounters?*

11) Has your *communicating relationship* with our Leader *renewed, strengthened, enabled,* and *inspired* you to reach out to others to fulfill His divine purpose?

In a nutshell:

Praise...seek...listen...praise...seek...listen...praise...seek...listen...

Hear...

Praise...seek...listen...

Confirmation...

Praise...seek...listen...

Act!

Praise!

CHAPTER 6

"OBEY MY WORD"

Part I—Walk In Christ

As we know the Lord better, He says, "Let's get moving!" Living and moving with the Lord is an adventure. You never know what's around the corner.

Paul was a man who loved the Lord and moved with Him. In Philippians 1:21, Paul said, "For to me, *to live is Christ,* and to die is gain." What an attitude!

Remember, Paul didn't meet Jesus in the flesh. He met Jesus through a supernatural experience on the road to Damascus (Acts 9). Then he received many spiritual *revelations* of Jesus, but not from any man's teaching (Gal. 1:11–23). His knowledge came through supernatural encounters.

If Jesus would reveal Himself to Paul in such powerful ways, then can't we expect the same, if our heart is as dedicated as Paul's was? Well, what if we're not that dedicated?

The Lord reveals Himself *to the degree we submit* to Him. He hasn't chosen anyone to be more important to

Him than another. He responds in proportion to our level of interest in and desire for Him. Not church activities, ministering to others, or any action on our part *for* Him, but our personal involvement *with* Him. Making Him the center of our lives.

From our relationship with Jesus comes a *lifestyle that reflects Him.* Others will be touched by His glory when we *walk in Him* as He lives in, around, and through us.

When I was a teenager and hadn't known the Lord very long, I had a terrifying dream that made a powerful impact on me. In the dream I was alone in a canyon with rock walls on all sides and no way out. Satan appeared in front of me and began slowly advancing to attack. I confidently spoke the word to him and told him to *go!* But he kept advancing closer and closer. I again spoke the word and told him to *be gone!* It didn't work…he kept coming closer. With my heart beating wildly within me, I instinctively screamed, *"Jesus!"*

All of a sudden Jesus emerged from within me and enveloped me like a force shield. When Satan saw Jesus surrounding me, he immediately disappeared.

I woke up with my heart still pounding, with the newfound realization that it is Jesus, as He lives within us, who provides His "force shield" as our protection.

As Jesus lives in us and we allow Him to live *through* us, our lives and the lives of others will be changed.

> As you therefore have received Christ Jesus the
> Lord, *so walk in Him,* having been firmly rooted
> and now being built up in Him and established

in your faith, just as you were instructed, and overflowing with gratitude. Colossians 2:6–7

"Head Honcho"

When I was little, I trusted my big brother Robert would take care of the bullies. When big kids in the neighborhood tried to scare us little ones, I confidently told them my big brother would beat them up! Of course he never had to, but it was reassuring to know I had someone big and strong that would protect me.

Our "big brother" is Jesus! "And in Him you have been made complete, and *He is the head over all rule and authority*" (Colossians 2:10). Many, if not most, people in the world would give anything they own to have a powerful big brother like Jesus. He fights our battles and rescues us when we trust Him to. And our big brother Jesus is head honcho. When you are head over all rule and authority, that's about as powerful as you can get!

In our walk with Him, we never need to be afraid of our enemies. Jesus will always take care of us, as we trust Him.

Righteousness by Faith

I used to think the word "righteous" meant sanctimonious or putting on "holy airs." I didn't know it actually means right-living stemming from purity of heart.

The bigger Jesus is in our lives, the purer our hearts

are. Then along comes right living, just like the train after the engine.

> More than that, I count all things to be loss in view of the surpassing value of knowing Christ Jesus my LORD, for whom I have suffered the loss of all things, and count them but rubbish in order that I may gain Christ, and may be found in Him, *not having a righteousness of my own* derived from the Law, *but that which is through faith in Christ, the righteousness which comes from God on the basis of faith*…Philippians 3:8–9

Only righteousness from God is pure and holy. Man's righteousness is never perfect or complete because we can't be truly right on our own. It says in the word that our righteousness is like filthy rags compared to the Lord's (Isaiah 64:6)!

One of the purposes of the laws given in the Old Testament was to show us we cannot measure up to the high standards of God without Him. When we try to be right and do right *on our own*, we either fall short of the high goals our Father sets for us, or if we make it, it's easy to become sanctimonious and self-righteous like the Pharisees.

Have you heard the songs that say, "I want to be more like Jesus"? Well, we do want to be more like Him, but we'll never achieve it in our own strength. Our righteousness comes and keeps on coming *from God* through our belief and faith that He is giving it to us as He dwells within us.

Got Jesus? Got righteousness!

Part II—Attitude of the Believer

Rejoice

Do you feel chipper and happy all the time? Ha ha ha! Of course not.

Philippians 4:4 says, *"Rejoice in the Lord always; again I will say, rejoice!"* We are not told to be happy all the time. We're told to *rejoice.* To rejoice means to be filled with joy. This verse is telling us to be filled with joy in the Lord *always.* Challenging, huh?

The joy of the Lord is not necessarily a "happy" feeling. It is a *gladness of heart stemming from an assurance of who the Lord is in our lives.*

Once when my friend Ann and I were praising, praying, and waiting on the Lord, He revealed, "Joy is a key to My eternal Kingdom. *Joy is the triumphant entry of victory."*

This told me if we are going to have victory in our lives, it enters in triumphantly through joy. Joy comes from knowing our Lord is the victor. And from knowing He is working all things together for our good because we love Him and are called according to His purpose (Romans 8:28).

We *must* maintain our joy. Even in the face of adversity, we must keep that gladness of heart, which comes from knowing the Lord is our protector and guide. Our all-sufficiency.

Praise is a vital ingredient in building and keeping the

joy of the Lord. The more we praise and worship Him, the more complete our joy and peace become.

So let's rejoice in the Lord always and let victory come in!

Be Anxious for Nothing

The Lord doesn't have to do anything for us. He *wants* to.

> *Be anxious for nothing,* but in everything by prayer and supplication with thanksgiving let your requests be made known to God.
> And the peace of God, which surpasses all comprehension, shall guard your hearts and your minds in Christ Jesus. Philippians 4:6–7

We are advised here to bring everything to God our Father by prayer and supplication. Supplications are humble and earnest requests. When we stay *humble, earnest, and thankful in our attitude toward our Lord, He will answer our prayers and guard us with His peace.*

The Merciful Heart

Exactly what is mercy? If you are merciful, you are kind, compassionate, and somewhat lenient. Giving mercy is offering more kindness than what justice requires.

I never used to care about mercy. I thought if people messed up, they should get what they deserved. Sounds kind of cold hearted, doesn't it?

I was glad for a little mercy on one family ski trip…

I was driving our family home to Florida from a weekend of skiing in North Carolina. It was getting late, the children had school the next morning, and I was going faster than the speed limit. When I saw blue lights flashing behind me, I knew with a sinking feeling that I was quite eligible for a speeding ticket. I said a quick prayer and pulled over with trepidation. The first police car pulled up behind me and was quickly joined by a second car. My dread mounted. The police officers informed me our vehicle was going ten miles per hour faster than the speedometer had shown. I knew I was in deep trouble then. After talking with me a few minutes, they said they just wanted to be sure we made it home safe from our trip and to slow down. Then let me go with a warning. That was definitely mercy!

> To sum up, let all be harmonious, sympathetic, brotherly, kindhearted, and humble in spirit; *not returning evil for evil, or insult for insult, but giving a blessing instead;* for you were called for the very purpose that you might inherit a blessing.
> 1 Peter 3:8–9

When I was growing up, my mother told us children on a regular basis, "Be ye kind one to another, tender hearted, forgiving one another, even as God for Christ's sake hath forgiven you" (Eph. 4:32, KJV). She would usually shorten it and tell us sternly, "Be ye kind!" I'm sure we needed the reminder.

The Lord not only wants us to be kind and brotherly

toward one another, but to do as He did and extend mercy to those who may not deserve it. Jesus told a story about a king who forgave the debt of his slave to illustrate this lesson (Matt. 18:21–35).

In the story, Jesus told about a king who forgave his slave's debt that was so large the slave would never have been able to repay it. Yet the same slave turned right around and mercilessly persecuted a fellow slave, who only owed him a little.

When the king found out his slave did not extend the same leniency that he had been granted, the king handed him over to the torturers! The king informed the merciless slave, "Should you not also have had mercy on your fellow slave, even as I had mercy on you?" (Matt. 18:33)

We expect the Lord to continue to forgive us all of our monstrous sins and yet many times we do not extend the same kind and lenient attitude toward our fellow man. It's especially hard to do when we feel like we've been wronged.

A merciful heart can be developed through Jesus Christ and an act of our will called self-control.

Now for this very reason also, applying all diligence, in your *faith* supply *moral excellence,* and in your moral excellence, *knowledge; and in your knowledge, self-control,* and in your self-control, *perseverance,* and in your perseverance, *godliness;* and in your godliness, *brotherly kindness,* and in your brotherly kindness, *love.* For if these qualities are yours and are increasing, they render you neither useless nor unfruitful in the true knowledge of our LORD Jesus Christ. 2 Peter 1:5–8

When we begin out of our *faith* with *moral excellence,* we are *starting* with excellent character or conduct according to God's standards of right and wrong. From our resulting *knowledge* of right and wrong, we are to exhibit *self-control* and *perseverance,* which brings *godliness.* It is only after we develop this godly lifestyle that true *brotherly kindness* and *love* come.

In 1 Peter 3:8–9, we are encouraged to be "harmonious, sympathetic, brotherly, kindhearted, and humble in spirit." These attributes come *after* we have developed our godly behavior through the knowledge of right and wrong, self-control and perseverance.

Through this godliness, our hearts will be softened and we'll be open to hear the cry of those who need our mercy.

Without a soft and compassionate heart, we're asking for trouble. Going back to the story of the king, Jesus said the king was so mad the servant didn't extend mercy, he handed him over to the torturers until he repaid all that was owed. Then Jesus said, *"So shall my heavenly Father also do to you, if each of you does not forgive his brother from your heart"* (Matt. 18:34–35).

It is very clear that we remove ourselves from the protection of the Lord when we have an unforgiving heart. We effectively walk right into the enemy's torture chamber and give them permission to put us on the racks!

We cannot afford to nurse our grievances and feel sorry for ourselves. Even if others have hurt us, we must extend mercy and forgive them. It is vital to our well-being. Our health and even our very lives may depend on it.

The "Broken" Contrite Heart

Okay, if you're like me, it's going to get a little tougher here...

On top of having a merciful heart, the Lord wants us *yielded* and *broken*. By broken, I don't mean in pieces, but like a horse is broken. Broken from a wild rebellious state into a tame and useable condition. Psalm 51:17 says, "The sacrifices of God are a *broken spirit; a broken and a contrite heart*, O God, Thou wilt not despise."

Here's where fasting and praying come in. They can help to "break" us. When you deny your flesh, your spirit and soul control your body. You in effect *"tame" your body to be in submission to your will.* Then the next step is *submitting your will to the Spirit of God* who dwells inside of you. It's a heck of a lot easier to hear what the Lord is trying to say to you when your body is not in control of your will and your spirit.

Food is the most common kind of fast, but we can fast many things. Television might be a good one for some people. The fast I feel led to the most is sweets. The Lord knows it's one of the greatest sacrifices for me!

Whatever you feel led to fast, keep these two things in mind: (1) Fasting is for *you*, it doesn't force God to do anything. (2) Fasting is a *reminder* to pray. Fasting without prayer doesn't accomplish much.

The soldier who is battle-ready is one who stands disciplined and yielded to his Commander-in-Chief. As soldiers in our Lord's army, we are submitted to Him in all things—body, mind, and spirit.

We can be prepared for battle at any time by living a disciplined, humble, and merciful life that says, "God first, me second." Then when we call, the Lord will answer and say, "Here I am" (Isaiah 58:9).

Stand Firm

The Lord expects us to build our lives upon His words.

> [Jesus said,] "Therefore everyone who *hears these words of Mine, and acts upon them,* may be compared to a wise man, who built his house upon the rock. And the rain descended, and the floods came, and the winds blew, and burst against that house; and yet it did not fall, for it had been founded upon the rock.
>
> "And everyone who *hears these words of Mine, and does not act upon them,* will be like a foolish man, who built this house upon the sand. And the rain descended, and the floods came, and the winds blew, and burst against that house; and it fell, and great was its fall." Matthew 7:24–27

As these scriptures say, when we base our lives upon

the word of the Lord, we build on a solid foundation that can support us in adversity. Conversely, when we do not *act* on His words, we do not have His solid support in times of trouble.

My friend Ann showed me the "t" in stand resembles a cross. If we remove the "t" from the word it leaves us with sand. The same thing happens when we remove the cross from our stand. It leaves us with an unsure foundation. There is nothing solid to build on.

> But let him *ask in faith without any doubting,* for the one who doubts is like the surf of the sea driven and tossed by the wind. For let not that man expect that he will receive anything from the LORD, being a double-minded man, unstable in all his ways. James 1:6–8

Examining this verse further, notice we should not expect to receive *anything* from the Lord when we are not single-mindedly standing firm in our belief and relationship with our Lord Jesus Christ.

The hand that wrote the book of James is most widely believed to be James, the brother of Jesus. James the son of Zebedee has also been brought forth as a possibility. Both of them were very close to our Lord Jesus Christ and were His disciples. Whichever one wrote it through the Holy Spirit did so from an intimate knowledge of how Jesus thought and responded. They lived, ate, and walked with Him daily. They knew Jesus required their total trust and confidence to receive from Him.

If they knew that about Jesus, we should learn from

them: having trust and confidence in Him to receive what we ask from Him; standing firm in our belief that He is moving on our behalf; acting on our belief in His words; and not wavering in our relationship with Him.

"Therefore, my beloved brethren whom I long to see, my joy and crown, so *stand firm in the Lord,* my beloved" (Philippians 4:1).

Part III—Behavior of the Believer

Put on the New Self

When the Lord is head honcho in our lives, He overflows into our behavior. Ask yourself, is He calling the shots, or are you? Is He guiding your responses to circumstances and people, or do you act first and then ask the Lord to "make it okay" afterward?

> But now you also, put them all aside: anger, wrath, malice, slander, and abusive speech from your mouth. Do not lie to one another, *since you laid aside the old self with its evil practices, and have put on the new self who is being renewed to a true knowledge according to the image of the One who created him.*
>
> And so, as those who have been chosen of God, holy and beloved, *put on a heart of compassion, kindness, humility, gentleness and patience; bearing with one another, and forgiving each other,* whoever has a complaint against anyone; just as the LORD forgave you, so also should you. *And beyond all*

these things put on love, which is the perfect bond of unity.

And let the peace of Christ rule in your hearts, to which indeed you were called in one body; and be thankful. Colossians 3:8–10, 12–15

As Paul writes in Colossians, we are being re-"newed" in the image of our Lord. When we put aside the way we were before Jesus became Lord of our lives and let him re-make us spiritually to be a reflection of Him, He shines through us with His compassion, kindness, humility, gentleness, and patience.

When we "put Him on" as it says, we're putting on His love and His peace. What a terrific new self we have in Christ Jesus!

Family Relations

Living in my family can be full of good times and bad times, but it's certainly never boring! Some of our family problems would be eliminated if we followed the order our Lord ordained for successful family units.

Wives, be subject to your husbands, as is fitting in the LORD.

Husbands, love your wives, and do not be embittered against them.

Children, be obedient to your parents in all things, for this is well-pleasing to the LORD.

Fathers, do not exasperate your children, that they may not lose heart. Colossians 3:18–21

In the same way, you *wives, be submissive to your own husbands* so that even if any of them are disobedient to the word, they may be won without a word by the behavior of their wives, as they observe your chaste and respectful behavior.

You *husbands likewise, live with your wives in an understanding way,* as with a weaker vessel, since she is a woman; and *grant her honor as a fellow heir of the grace of life, so that your prayers may not be hindered.*

To sum up, let all be harmonious, sympathetic, brotherly, kindhearted, and humble in spirit; not returning evil for evil, or insult for insult, but giving a blessing instead; for you were called for the very purpose that you might inherit a blessing.
1 Peter 3:1–2, 7–9

Ouch! Some of that is pretty hard to do!

Families are very special relationships that require more acceptance and love than most. Our family units are supposed to be miniature versions of our heavenly Father's family.

The holy family, or Trinity, adores and respects each other. They know they each have a tremendously important role. The Father proclaims what is to be done, the Son gives the word to bring it about, and the Holy Spirit is the power that causes it to happen. Each one is dependant upon the other to do their part.

In our earthly families, God wants us to love, support, and depend on one another. He designed each one of us to have specific roles and responsibilities within the family unit.

The Bible tells us the husband/father role is to be submissive to God. The wife/mother is to be under her husband's protective covering and God's. The children are to be under the parents' authority and protection and also submissive to God.

Without God as the head of the house, no perfect order will be established, and the family unit will suffer. Subsequently, when the child or the woman in the home doesn't place themselves under the covering that God has ordained, the family will not function as the Lord intends.

Don't confuse being under the authority and protection of the next family member in the "chain of command," with being *less than* that person. We are equally joint heirs with Christ. But that doesn't mean that we are alike or have the same jobs to do.

The parents need to train their children without provoking them. The children should respond with respect and obedience. If the wife does it right, she'll honor her husband with respect and submission. Whereas, the husband's role is to love his wife as much as Christ loves the church. That means loving her enough to sacrifice his desires if need be.

A pastor I once knew said he felt the only way men learn how to place themselves under submission to the Lord was to see it in their wives as they submitted to them. For many reasons, the family structure works when we follow the Lord's instruction.

If you're like most of us, this may sound tough to do all the time. We absolutely can't do it without love. Only love helps us truly surrender our will to another.

Love is crucial, but to honor and respect one another is also vital for the success of the family. Even if a wife or children submit all day long to the father/husband, there will be no lasting happiness in the home if the father/husband doesn't return the honor with love and cherish them.

I resisted this structure for years, not wanting to relinquish any "control." When I finally decided to honor my husband as head of our home under God's direction and change my attitude toward "who's the boss," our home became much more harmonious. It also began a much deeper mutual trust that was not in our marriage before.

Today we hear stories of shocking abuse in the family, so I must add an exception for anyone who may be living with really destructive behaviors in the family. First and foremost, being led by the Lord is crucial to finding your way out of this kind of battleground. Healthy, God-inspired boundaries may need to be employed to effect healing before a normal family environment can exist. This is the time to call on your fellow soldiers for emotional and spiritual guidance. Together we can make it out of this snare of the enemy, to find the correct ways to submit to one another.

Jesus showed us how to surrender to the Father's will. As we allow Him to lead us, He will guide us to submit in the right way for our circumstances. Then we can trust that love and honor will be returned to us, full circle.

Fellow Workers

My husband and I used to own a fast-paced rental business that we gave our blood, sweat, and tears to for years. We put in a tremendous number of hours ourselves and expected our employees to work hard as well. In the first few years of being in business, our co-laborers would teasingly call our business the "slave center"!

Employee and employer can easily be substituted for the words slave and master in the following passages, for Paul was referring to work attitudes.

> Slaves, in all things *obey those who are your masters on earth,* not with external service, as those who merely please men, but *with sincerity of heart,* fearing the LORD. Whatever you do, *do your work heartily, as for the LORD* rather than for men; knowing that from the LORD you will receive the reward of the inheritance. It is the LORD Christ whom you serve. For he who does wrong will receive the consequences of the wrong which he has done, and that without partiality.
>
> Masters, *grant to your slaves justice and fairness,* knowing that you too have a Master in heaven. Col. 3:22–25, 4:1

When we do our work heartily, it's an important witness to the unsaved world. It shows we will be the best that we can be regardless of man's recognition. To unselfishly give of ourselves in our jobs is an important statement of what Christ Jesus is doing in our lives. It can be a door to share how Jesus has changed and enhanced our lives.

Whether we work for others or for ourselves, to be fair and honest in all of our business dealings is imperative for the Christian walk. The Lord requires a "balanced scale." The "weights" need to be the same on the giving and receiving ends. Our job is to deal fairly with everyone and give them good value for their money if we offer goods or services.

To reflect Christ Jesus is our goal—even in our work. What would He do?

Share with the Brethren

It's not very hard to share when you love someone, is it? How about when you don't know them? It gets a little harder, doesn't it? That's because people by nature are selfish. It's only as we love that we want to share.

When the Lord's love is shining through us, we'll want to share what we have with our brothers and sisters in Christ like they did in the first church... "And all those who had believed were together, and had all things in common; and they began selling their property and possessions, *and were sharing them with all, as anyone might have need*" (Acts 2:44–45).

Wow! We certainly have a long way to go to be as unselfish as the first believers. If we practiced this today, we would be accused of everything from way-out cultists to communists! Our society full of the world's greed would not understand the simple and unselfish love that puts others' needs equivalent to or above our own.

Jesus does not usually require us to give up everything we own. He said if we have two coats, share one (Luke 3:11). In Acts 4:34, it says all who were owners of land or houses (plural) would sell them and donate them to the needy. God would have us be generous, not strip ourselves down to where we are the needy ones.

Once in awhile I have seen exceptions to this when He is teaching someone a lesson about faith, or maybe pride. Then He may ask them to give everything away as a mechanism to stretch and grow.

I saw the Lord require my brother to sell his expensive home in an exclusive neighborhood and give up every expensive toy he owned one by one, as He prepared Robert to leave creature comforts to minister to the Indians in New Mexico. This is not the norm for most Christians, however.

Some believers think they *have* to be poor to be humble and act godly. The problem is, poor people have less to bless others with. They can certainly give of themselves, which is wonderful, but that won't feed a starving child!

I believe we should desire to be people of abundance for the purpose of blessing others. Living a life of plenty is not sinful. The more we have, the more we can give. What is wrong is to have much and not share with those in need. But even in our sharing we must seek the Lord.

He wants to guide us concerning who to give to, what to give, and when to give it.

Years ago, I had a precious Christian housekeeper, who seemed to always be having money troubles. Once she wanted to borrow some money from me, so I prayed about it and I felt impressed to give her a particular amount of money.

After that she asked me nearly every week for extra money for different needs. I gave it to her for a few weeks, until the Lord put a check in my spirit about giving her any more money. When I prayed about it, I believe the Lord said in my spirit, "*I told you to give her money once. You have given her more money, and now she is looking to you as her source instead of to Me.*" It seems when we give without His guidance, it isn't very pleasing to Him. We don't know the whole picture; He does.

With the Lord's guidance, we can take care of our Christian brothers and sisters and not see them in need. If we all give the makings of one simple meal each week to a local church "food pantry," what a difference it would make. Also giving our outgrown, not outworn clothes to a church "clothes closet" would go a long way toward clothing our needy brethren.

If you've ever traveled to a foreign country, you have quickly seen how rich Americans are in relation to most of the world. We throw away more of our abundance than we give away. My heart's desire is to see a "Christian helping Christian" program become common among the various churches. If we posted "Have a Gift" listings from people with items to donate (furniture, baby items, etc.), and "Have a Need" listings from those with specific needs, we could bless each other and eliminate needs, much like the church of the first century.

As we are sensitive to the Lord's leading, we'll give to our fellow soldiers the right gift at the right time. Not too much, not too little. This fortifies the army, and we'll be blessed as givers and receivers.

> You yourselves know that these hands ministered to my own needs and to the men who were with me. In everything I showed you that *by working hard in this manner you must help the weak* and remember the words of the LORD Jesus, that He Himself said, "*It is more blessed to give than to receive.*" Acts 20:34–35

Be Watchful for False Teachers

With today's lightning quick news coverage, we've seen the appalling exposure of immorality and deceit in too many prominent personalities. We act like it's something new and shocking, but there has been and always will be "wolves in sheep's clothing."

> But false prophets also arose among the people, just as *there will also be false teachers among you,* who will secretly introduce destructive heresies, even denying the Master who bought them, bringing swift destruction upon themselves. And many will follow their sensuality, and because of them

> the way of the truth will be maligned; and in their greed they will exploit you with false words; their judgment from long ago is not idle, and their destruction is not asleep. 2 Peter 2:1–3

Some religious leaders may start off with the intention of following Jesus, but for various reasons get off His track. Some may be motivated by greed or power. Many just aren't mature enough to deal with temptation and walk away unscathed. These seem to be the most newsworthy, but in my opinion aren't the most harmful.

What is far more damaging to the body are teachers and preachers who mislead congregations with false and/ or incomplete doctrine. When leaders deny the power of God for our lives, they fulfill the scripture that says, "… holding to a form of godliness (religion), although they have denied its power; and avoid such men as these" (2 Tim. 3:5). These are harmful to our position against the enemy when they teach us to deny the power of God in the world today. When we deny the Holy Spirit's power, we are power*less* before the enemy. That is just how our enemy wants us. Defeated.

God's power comes through His Holy Spirit today, just like it did when the scriptures were written. He said, "For I, the Lord, do not change…" (Mal. 3:6).

God hasn't gotten to our century and decided, "Oops! That power stuff is sort of old fashioned; I think I'll do away with it." No, no, no. The way He was in yester years is how He is today. I don't think He has any plans of changing in the future either.

I grew up in a church that believed the power that was transferred to the first disciples died with them. They didn't believe God wanted us to have power like the first disciples had. Consequently, when people got sick, the ones who weren't healed by modern medicine died. They accepted their problems stoically and looked forward to leaving this world and going to heaven one day. They lived without knowledge of the power of God for today, because the leaders didn't know the truth in that area.

The enemy works hard trying to keep leaders in the dark concerning the power of God. Some leaders haven't been exposed to the knowledge concerning God's power. Some have been exposed, but for some reason didn't understand or like what they saw because it was unusual. Others don't want to accept it because it would mean what they have believed was wrong, and they don't want to be wrong. And there are the ones who are jealous of other ministries who are greater than their own, and so they criticize with eyes of suspicion.

Teachers who are rooted in God's word will bear the fruit of the Spirit. In discerning whether someone is full of the Lord and teaching His unadulterated word, we can look at their fruit. What is coming forth from their lives? How about their ministry?

Next, when we are familiar with what the word of God says, we can analyze teaching to see if it lines up with Scripture. If we don't know what the word says, we could be drawn off base by something that may sound good, but isn't consistent with the word.

We have to be vigilant to watch for false teachers. But

when we see and hear unscriptural things from teachers in our army, don't persecute them. Pray for them! Seek the Lord to see if some of the brethren should *lovingly* try to get them on the right path.

I have seen too many people crucified and pushed out of a body of believers. That is not the way of the Lord. *He always corrects—then restores.*

However, if the false teacher is unrepentant, avoid them and know that God's judgment is perfect.

"You therefore, beloved, knowing this beforehand, *be on your guard* lest, being carried away by the error of unprincipled men, you fall from your own steadfastness" (2 Peter 3:17).

Christ Is Head of the Body

The scripture tells us that figuratively, Christ is head of the body. We, the church, are His body today. Is the arm arguing with the foot? And the shoulder disagreeing with the knee?

> Therefore let no one act as your judge in regard to food or drink or in respect to a festival or a new moon or a Sabbath day—things which are a mere shadow of what is to come; but the substance (body—KJV) belongs to Christ. Colossians 2:16–17

The body of Christ has become so diverse and segregated by individual doctrine there is no real unity in it today. Because various denominations perceive the scripture somewhat differently, there has developed division in the church.

We are all probably missing it to some degree in at least one area, if not more. I think some scripture, particularly dealing with end times, is veiled intentionally by God so we will continue to be dependant upon Him for the answers.

Whether or not we're right about what God wants in His church, we should be tolerant of each other's perception and understanding of the word. If we have His love operating in us, we will move into *unity* by the power of the Holy Spirit.

Because there are different customs and traditions in various denominations, we may come together to worship a little differently from place to place. We should not focus on our differences, but on the common ground we as Christians have.

Our belief in Jesus Christ as head of the church, along with God the Father and our precious Holy Spirit, should be of paramount importance. Loving our holy Family— Father, Son and Holy Spirit—with all of our heart, mind, and soul, and loving our "neighbor," who may be anyone that comes across our path, is true Christianity (Matthew 22:37–40).

Using the Bible as our handbook and allowing the Holy Spirit to guide and direct us comes next. If we do these things first the differences will not be too important.

If you hear something that doesn't line up with the word, leave it alone. But still walk in love with your brother! As Jesus said, "Do not judge lest you be judged.

For in the way you judge, you will be judged; and by your standard of measure, it shall be measured to you." (Matt. 7:1–2).

If we keep the Bible as our guide and Christ as Lord of our lives, the love that emanates from Him through us will manifest itself in unity throughout the body of the church. Then judgment and criticism will be replaced by a loving tolerance and acceptance of our differences.

Wisdom Toward Outsiders

My mother gave me a book by Joyce Meyer called *Me and My Big Mouth.* What do you suppose my mother was trying to tell me?

When I was younger, I would offer my opinion to whoever would listen. I knew I had good judgment and thought I was right, at least most of the time! My sister Carol wisely advised that many times there is more than one right way to do something. She challenged me, "Why don't you count and see how many times you can let other people be right?" I was stunned at how I must have come across to others.

I meekly decided I needed to change the way I communicated. My aunt Marian is always so affirming, I decided to emulate some of the ways she shares with others. In the past I would say, "I think you should do this or the other." Now I try to ask, "What do you think about doing this or the other?" Suggesting instead of pushing sure makes a big difference in how ideas are received and welcomed!

Conduct yourselves with wisdom toward outsiders, making the most of the opportunity. *Let your speech always be with grace, seasoned, as it were, with salt, so that you may know how you should respond to each person.* Colossians 4:5–6

In cooking we adjust the amount of salt we use to the food and to personal taste. Like in cooking, we should *adjust our conversation* to respond to the needs and interest level of the people we meet. If you share Christ with others, you want your words to be received, so each witness should be unique to that individual. We don't need a "canned" approach to share Jesus. Just an openness to share at the right time what He has done for you.

Aunt Bunky once told me, "If you have beautiful hair, you don't need to go around telling everyone, 'I have beautiful hair!' They will come to you and ask, 'How do you get your hair to be so beautiful?' The same thing applies to witnessing for Jesus. If who He is in your life *shows,* then people will want to know what you have that makes you so special."

When Jesus is the salt in your life, He'll show you how much "seasoning" each conversation and witness should have.

Secret of Getting Along

I think a real tragedy that occurred during the "faith movement" was the misunderstanding that many people had concerning finances and needs. So many heard the promises that are scattered throughout the scriptures and replaced the word "need" with "want" and missed what God was really saying.

"And my God *shall supply all your needs* according to His riches in glory in Christ Jesus" (Philippians 4:19). Our Lord says He will take care of us and will be sure that we have a sufficiency of all we *need*. When we walk close to Him and are obedient to Him and His word, He will provide for us with a generosity that can be truly amazing.

Contrary to some teaching I've heard, He will not drop buckets of money in our laps even if, as some suggest, we give away all of our money! Normally He blesses our *hard work* with a "bountiful harvest."

> I know how to get along with humble means, and I also know how to live in prosperity; in any and every circumstance I have learned the secret of being filled and going hungry, both of having abundance and suffering need. *I can do all things through Him who strengthens me.* Philippians 4:12–13

Sometimes our enemy may come along to try and steal what God has blessed us with. Then we need to do as Paul suggests and press in to Christ more deeply and allow Him to strengthen us, to regain the ground that was stolen.

Remember, our Father has riches beyond our wildest imagination. He is capable of, and desires to bless His children with *all* that we *need*. He also likes to give presents and may surprise us with gifts. He knows what

He should and shouldn't give us according to His great wisdom.

Generally, the more we give to the Lord, the more He gives back in return, but don't give to *get!* The Lord does not bless greedy motives.

Give because you love Him and want to provide for others. Give because you want to see the gospel spread. Give because the Holy Spirit impresses you to. *But don't give because you think you have to for the Lord to give back in return.* He sees our hearts. We can't fool Him! He wants us to give because we *want* to. Cheerfully! Even if we only give a small portion of our "harvest" (tithe), He will open the windows of heaven and pour out a blessing that we can't even contain (Malachi 3:10).

> [Jesus said,] "Give, and it will be given to you; good measure, pressed down, shaken together, running over, they will pour into your lap. *For by your standard of measure it will be measured to you in return.*" Luke 6:38

As the Word Dwells Within You

When the word is a big part of our lives, it bursts forth in interesting ways.

> *Let the word of Christ richly dwell within you,* with all wisdom *teaching and admonishing one another* with psalms and hymns and spiritual songs, *singing with thankfulness* in your hearts to God. And whatever you do in word or deed, *do all* in

the name of the LORD Jesus, *giving thanks* through Him to God the Father. Colossians 3:16–17

As His life and words become a part of us they will blossom forth into mature spiritual responses in our lives. We'll also have His wisdom to know how to bring others up in the Lord.

What is the word producing in *you?*

Part IV—Walk by the Spirit

What do you think of when I say, "Holy Spirit"? Do you think of a vague, shapeless, mysterious being, like I thought He was when I was young?

But I say, *walk by the Spirit, and you will not carry out the desire of the flesh.* For the flesh sets its desire against the Spirit, and the Spirit against the flesh; for these are in opposition to one another, so that you may not do the things that you please. But if you are led by the Spirit, you are not under the Law. Galatians 5:16–18

Because the Holy Spirit is everywhere at once, He can be difficult to picture in our minds. The Bible doesn't state that He has a particular form, but it does give many of His attributes that help us know Him as a real person.

He is our *Teacher, Helper* and *Comforter* (1 Cor. 2:10–13, John 14:16–26), and our *Guide into all truth* (John 16:13). He also *lives within us* as believers (Rom. 8:11). As He makes His home within us, he *gives us power* (Mic.

3:8), *sanctifies us* (Rom. 15:16), and *gives us joy, peace,* and *righteousness* (Rom. 14:17).

The Holy Spirit is a wonderful fellow and He wants to be *your* friend.

Our Helper

When Jesus was preparing His followers for His imminent departure, He tried to explain a little about the role the Holy Spirit would play in their lives:

> "But I tell you the truth, it is to your advantage that I go away; for *if I do not go away, the Helper shall not come to you; but if I go, I will send Him to you.*
>
> "And He, when He comes, will convict the world concerning sin, and righteousness, and judgment; concerning sin, because they do not believe in Me; and concerning righteousness, because I go to the Father, and you no longer behold Me; and concerning judgment, because the ruler of this world has been judged.
>
> "I have many more things to say to you, but you cannot bear them now. But *when He, the Spirit of truth, comes, He will guide you into all the truth;* for He will not speak on His own initiative, but whatever He hears, He will speak; and *He will disclose to you what is to come. He shall glorify Me;* for *He shall take of Mine, and shall disclose it to you.* All things that the Father has are Mine; therefore

I said, that He takes of Mine, and will disclose it to you." John 16:7–15

The Holy Spirit reveals Jesus and our precious heavenly Father to us. *We need to have a relationship with Him as a person.* He deserves it!

The Holy Spirit has widely been ignored in many churches, through lack of knowledge, or the mistaken belief that His only purpose is to reveal Jesus and our Father to us. The truth is, even though one of His jobs is to glorify Jesus, He has much more to offer.

First and foremost He wants to be our *friend.* It's difficult to help someone, comfort them, and guide and teach them if you don't have a close relationship with them. He wants us to get to know Him.

After reading about Benny Hinn's relationship with the Holy Spirit in his book, *Good Morning Holy Spirit,* I realized the Holy Spirit was a person who thought and felt and was sent here to be my helper.

Up until then I prayed (or bossed might be a better word), "Holy Spirit, help me to pray as I ought, for today." I knew this was scriptural (Romans 8:26–27), and I believed He would perform as the word dictates.

It began to dawn on me that I had been commanding God the Holy Spirit to perform the word instead of *asking* Him humbly to do it for me. I was so ashamed! After apologizing profusely, I was determined to seek the Holy Spirit for His friendship and guidance.

When my household settled down for the night, I secluded myself in a quiet room. I sat cross-legged on the daybed and closed my eyes to seek Him. I whispered, "Holy Spirit, I want you to be my friend. Will you let me get to know you?"

As I sat there in the hushed stillness of the room, I began to feel a warm glowing heat upon my skin. The sensation reminded me of times when I was very sunburned and heat radiated from my skin. The peculiar difference was this heat was radiating *onto* my skin instead of from it. The warmth moved like currents of air revolving around me. His peace enveloped me like warm, fluffy cotton. All I could do was smile and thank Him for answering me in such a precious way.

There was a question I had been wondering about for some time, so I decided to ask my newfound Teacher about it. I asked, "Holy Spirit, I've never understood who really lives inside of me. Some places in the Bible say that you do and other places say that Jesus does. If Jesus is seated at the right hand of the Father, how can He live in me? How does all of that work?"

As I sat patiently waiting, I began to see a picture. I saw earth as viewed from out in space. I could see two beams of light originating from one point on earth, going to two separate points in space (like a V shape). All of a sudden I understood this signified the Holy Spirit who is the one on earth at this time, reveals the Father (one point in space) and Jesus (the other point in space) *through Himself* (the point on earth and all the light in between). It kind of reminded me of the old Star Trek shows where people were transported through the beam of light. I could see that as we have the Holy Spirit's indwelling, Jesus can live in us and we can go into our Father's presence because the Holy Spirit is in all places at once. He is like the transporter.

Our precious, gentle Holy Spirit is vital to our relationship with our heavenly Family, for He is our communicator. He is also so much more. Get to know Him. Walk with Him. He is waiting!

Baptism in the Holy Spirit

One of the big religious controversies in the church is the belief of what can, should, or might happen when we receive the baptism of the Holy Spirit.

The Greek meaning of baptize is to immerse or bathe. So when we are baptized in the Holy Spirit, we should expect to be *totally drenched in Him.* Jesus said to expect this second baptism, the first being in water (Acts 1:5).

The question in hot debate is: What is the *evidence* that we have received this special baptism? Many say that you must speak in tongues (the ability to speak in various languages given as a supernatural gift) as the first disciples did at Pentecost. Others say that speaking in tongues was a unique miracle only for the first disciples and is not evidence of the baptism of the Holy Spirit. Folks, this should be a minor issue.

Jesus said when we are filled with the Holy Spirit we shall *receive power* and we should be witnesses for Him wherever we go... "But *you shall receive power* when the Holy Spirit has come upon you; and you shall be My witnesses both in Jerusalem, and in all Judea and Samaria, and even to the remotest part of the earth" (Acts 1:8). His power helps us be effective witnesses for Him.

We need to see if we have the *power* of the Holy Spirit operating in our lives as a checkpoint for the level of His infilling.

If you won a prize in a contest and you never went to claim it, you would never get the prize, would you? Likewise, if you never ask the Lord to manifest His power through you, He will not push it on you. He is a gentleman and waits patiently for us to come to Him.

We should desire all of the gifts and should let Him know it. But realize that He gives us spiritual gifts as He chooses, for the common good (1 Cor. 12:7,11). He will usually give them to us if our motives are pure and He feels we are ready to handle them.

If we ask for all His gifts and don't see the manifestation of a particular gift, then continue to stand in faith for it. When He has prepared us to receive it, then we'll operate in it.

The gifts of the Spirit are: the word of wisdom, the word of knowledge, faith, gifts of healing, effecting of miracles, prophecy, distinguishing of spirits, various kinds of languages (also called tongues), and the interpretation of such languages or tongues (1 Cor. 12:8–10). These are the gifts of *power*.

Do you have any power gifts operating in you? If not, why not ask Him right now for a fresh infilling of the Holy Spirit? You'll be glad you did!

Grieving the Holy Spirit

Once the Holy Spirit gives us a gift, He never takes it back (Romans 11:29). But if we grieve Him, He becomes very still.

If you have ever been in a gathering of Christians and the Holy Spirit was very active, you probably saw some interesting things. Many times, I've seen people so overcome with His power they couldn't stand up. One Rodney Howard Brown meeting I was in, people laughed in waves. The laughter started in one area and would sweep across the congregation in a rhythmic pattern. I had perma-grin during this meeting and felt so weighted down with a blanket of peacefulness, I couldn't get out of my chair for quite awhile. Other times, people have gotten Holy Spirit surgery and come away completely healed. The list is endless and amazingly cool if you are open-minded.

The Holy Spirit's power is evident when He *moves*. We definitely want Him to move in our lives. No movement, no power operating in our lives.

What causes Him to become still?

> And do not grieve the Holy Spirit of God, by whom you were sealed for the day of redemption. Let all *bitterness and wrath and anger and clamor and slander* be put away from you, along with all *malice.* Eph. 4:30–31

This passage suggests some of the attitudes that offend our Holy Spirit. I am sure there are more nasty behaviors that offend Him, but the idea here is that He can be grieved with our negative behavior. We really don't want to grieve our Helper, Comforter, and Guide into all truth. We need Him!

Fruit of the Spirit

Are you fruity? When we have the Holy Spirit living in us, people can tell by the fruit we bear. Just like an apple tree bears apples, the Holy Spirit bears fruit after His kind.

"But the fruit of the Spirit is *love, joy, peace, patience, kindness, goodness, faithfulness, gentleness, self-control;* against such things there is no law" (Galatians 5:22–23).

All of the fruit of the Spirit originate from His love. Remember, God *is* love (1 John 4:8). Because of *love* we have the remaining fruit:

1) Joy is love's strength.

2) Peace is love's security.

3) Patience is love's endurance.

4) Kindness is love's conduct.

5) Goodness is love's character.

6) Faithfulness is love's confidence.

7) Gentleness is love's humility.

8) Self-control is love's victory.[13]

What kind of fruit do you have on your branches?

Through Love...

Have you ever noticed that God's spiritual laws seem to be opposite of the world's view of the right order of things?

> The world says, "Show me Jesus first and then I will believe."
> The Bible says, "We must *believe first* on the Lord Jesus Christ and then we are saved."
> The world says, "Let me see what happens and then I will say that it did."
> The Lord says, "*Speak forth the word* and then it will happen."
> The world says, "I will forgive you if you love me first."
> The word says, "*Love first* and then *you* will be forgiven."

It doesn't change anything to question the order of God's spiritual laws. He made them that way for a purpose. Instead we need to learn them like a new subject in school.

These laws may seem backward at first, but then as they become a part of us, we begin to see *the world has become backward from God's laws.* Unlearning old habits and thought patterns is the new challenge!

Even though the love of the Lord will shine through us if He resides in us, we still have a will. We have to *make a choice* to forgive someone who has wronged us.

We have to choose to walk in love, then allow the Lord to reflect His love through us.

The pure, God kind of love is one of the biggest keys in our Lord's kingdom. Got to have it to be properly prepared for battle and have our prayers unhindered.

Love perfects everything we do in the spiritual realm. It makes up for our deficiencies and covers a multitude of sins (1 Peter 4:8).

Love is one of the weapons of our warfare. The enemy can't stand it and is ultimately destroyed by it. The opposing forces try *very hard* to draw us off our love stance. *Don't give in* to unforgiving attitudes and hatred. If we do, it can cause us to lose our battles because we won't be walking with and in Christ.

Even as love perfects us, it also perfects the spiritual laws. For example, we can bake a beautiful cake without sugar but it won't taste very good. So love is to spiritual law. We need it to complete the effectiveness.

Galatians 5:6 tells us our faith works through love... "For in Christ Jesus neither circumcision nor uncircumcision means anything, but *faith working through love*." As our love surrounds our faith, it becomes truly pleasing to God.

We can have faith and other spiritual gifts without love. But without love we are nothing... "And if I have the gift of prophecy, and know all mysteries and all knowledge; *and if I have all faith, so as to remove mountains, but do not have love, I am nothing*" (1 Cor. 13:2).

It is through love we serve one another and bear one another's burdens...

Brethren, even if a man is caught in any trespass, you who are spiritual, restore such a one in a spirit of gentleness; each one looking to yourself, lest you too be tempted. *Bear one another's burdens, and thus fulfill the law of Christ.* Galatians 6:1–2

Do not be deceived, God is not mocked; *for whatever a man sows, this he will also reap.* For the one who sows to his own flesh shall from the flesh reap corruption, but the one who sows to the Spirit shall from the Spirit reap eternal life. And let us not lose heart in doing good, for in due time we shall reap if we do not grow weary. So then, while we have opportunity, *let us do good to all men, and especially to those who are of the household of the faith.* Galatians 6:7–10

Let's support one another even as Christ supports us. Love one another even as He loves us. And do good to one another even as He is *so good* to us.

CHECKLIST

1) Have you learned to *rejoice* in the Lord in *all* things?

2) Have you cast your cares upon the Lord and are *anxious for nothing?*

3) Are you *showing mercy* when the opportunity presents itself?

4) Have you allowed the Lord to "*break*" you? Do you "*break yourself*" through prayer and fasting?

5) Are you *standing firm* on the Rock?

6) Have you put away fleshly things and *put on the new self?*

7) Are your *family relations* modeled after our heavenly Family?

8) Is Christ reflected in your work and *relationship with fellow workers?*

9) Are you *sharing with those in need?* Especially your brothers and sisters in Christ?

10) Are you *watchful for false teachers?* Are you praying for them?

11) Are you *tolerant* of your brother's differences?

12) Is Christ the "*salt*" of your conversation?

13) Are you *giving* to the Lord *cheerfully?* Are you *asking what* He wants you to give *and when?*

14) As the Word dwells within you, are you *teaching and encouraging others* and *singing about Him and to Him?*

15) Do you *know the Holy Spirit?*

16) What kind of *fruit* do you have on your spiritual branches?

17) Are you *walking in love?*

18) Do you *support and do good* to others?

The Lord has called us to *obey His word,* particularly in our lifestyle as believers and soldiers in His army. We cannot expect to pick out the parts in His holy word that we like and ignore the rest. When we train in His camp, it has to be by His rules, not ours.

When we acknowledge who our General is and abide by His instruction, our march in the ranks will be in unison not only with our fellow soldiers, but also with our Commanding General who leads us to win the war!

CHAPTER 7

"HEARKEN UNTO MY VOICE"

Part I—Commitment

Repentance

Nobody likes to hear, "Repent!" I know this isn't the fun stuff, but we gotta know about it, and we gotta do it.

There are two perceptions of repentance. The world thinks repentance is regret for doing something wrong. Repentance really means to sincerely regret a sin and also to *turn away* from the wrong behavior. *Regret without change is not true repentance.* An "I'm sorry" followed by doing the same stupid thing over again doesn't get it!

Once we turn away from former bad behavior, we should also turn away from guilt. When we allow Jesus to cover us, His blood soaks up our guilt and declares us "Not Guilty" before our Father. He is so merciful He doesn't punish us for breaking His commandments, but simply "washes us clean" and sends us on our way to love and serve through Him (Heb. 9:11–28).

As Jesus atones, cleanses, and makes us right through

the spiritual covering of His blood, our loving heavenly Father *forgives* and *forgets* our transgressions (Jer. 31:33–34). He simply chooses to not remember our sin anymore!

We are the ones who do the remembering—and the enemy helps us dwell on it with guilt and condemnation. When this happens we should resist these thoughts with the word, for we are now righteous through Christ (Philippians 3:9).

Many times something I have seen or heard will trigger a memory from my self-indulgent past and things I'm ashamed of have haunted me with guilt. I've had to learn to cover my thoughts with the spiritual blood of Jesus. He then miraculously cleanses my thoughts and the guilt goes away. Praise God!

The only time the Lord seems to remind me of my past is when I've been critical or unforgiving. He gently *convicts* me that He forgave me of a lot, so I should also forgive like He does.

Checkpoint: (1) The enemy *condemns.* They want us to feel unworthy, trapped, guilty, afraid, or angry. (2) The Lord *convicts.* There is always a way out with the Lord, *redemption!*

The Humble Heart

Felt humble lately?

"...and if My people who are called by My name *humble themselves and pray, and seek My face and turn from their wicked ways,* then I will hear from heaven, will forgive their sin, and will heal their land." 2 Chronicles 7:14

After we turn from our sinful ways with true repentance, the next step we take is a *humbling of ourselves*. This isn't a real popular idea since we've grown up in a society where pride is associated with strength. We've been taught that if we are humble, we are weak and foolish doormats.

Actually the opposite is true. When we choose as an act of our will to get out of the superiority mode, it takes strength and determination to do it! Boy, it takes a lot of strength!

When we choose to make ourselves less and the Lord more, He begins to exalt us as He wills... "But the greatest among you shall be your servant. And *whoever exalts himself shall be humbled*; and *whoever humbles himself shall be exalted*" (Matthew 23:11–12).

Humility shouldn't be confused with self-abasement, where people degrade themselves. Our goal is to recognize who the Great One really is and to not have false pride in ourselves. When we give Him the glory and not ourselves, He will lift us up and cause us to be mighty in His kingdom.

Dedication

Commitment? Dedication? What's the difference?

Believe it or not, there's a big difference between commitment and dedication. To *commit* is to bind or involve oneself or to pledge,[14] and to *dedicate* is to give up

HEARKEN UNTO MY VOICE

wholly or earnestly for some purpose or person.[15] We are to do both in our walk with the Lord.

To commit is *to choose* to make Jesus Lord of our lives in every area. It is *making a conscious decision* that we will follow our Leader and not our own desires. *To decide* to seek His will in every circumstance. This is commitment.

Dedication is the *act* of that commitment. It is the *follow-through* and the *acting out* of wholehearted surrender and obedience to the Lord.

Who will we follow each day? Me, myself, and I, or the Lord? Choose the winner—Jesus our King.

> Trust in the LORD, and do good; dwell in the land and cultivate faithfulness. Delight yourself in the LORD; and He will give you the desires of your heart. *Commit your way to the LORD,* trust also in Him, and He will do it. And He will bring forth your righteousness as the light, and your judgment as the noonday. Psalms 37:3–6

The Orchestra

Ever thought of yourself as an instrument?

When I was preparing to introduce a new program to the women in our church, I sought the Lord about what He wanted to do with us. During my prayer, I saw a picture of an orchestra taking shape, but all the instruments were people! Then I could see the back of the conductor who I perceived was the Lord, and He was leading the orchestra in a beautiful symphony. They were divided into three sections: (1) the tambourines and cymbals, (2) the harps and lyres, and (3) the trumpets and horns.

He showed me I was like a trumpet or horn. People like me are the ones who *proclaim His word* (prophets, evangelists, preachers, and teachers). As I've mentioned before, my name in Hebrew means "lily." A lily is shaped like a trumpet and symbolizes a trumpet in some scripture.

Then I could see my friend Ann was like a harp. The harps and lyres are the ones who *offer up His praises* (singers, musicians, and dancers).

My thoughts then turned to a good friend Eleanor who I could see was like a cymbal. The cymbals and tambourines are those who are primarily involved with the *work of the Lord.*

We may fit into more than one category because of what we do, but I believe if you ask the Lord what instrument you are, He will show you one that is predominantly you.

There is a place for each of us in the Lord's orchestra. He has a seat reserved with your name on it. *He needs each one of us to "play" our part for the whole orchestra to perform, as it should.* Without *you* the orchestra will not be complete.

Which instrument are you? Take your seat and let's play our parts for His glory!

Part II—Follow-through—Godly Living

The Beginning of Wisdom

Want to be a wise guy?

Fear and reverence of the Lord is the beginning of wisdom (Prov. 1:7). People don't talk much about fearing the Lord anymore. We hear more of the "snuggle up close and feel the love" kind of messages than the "fire and brimstone" kind of messages we used to hear years ago. The truth of the matter is God is all-powerful and we should have a healthy respect for the being that can if He so desires, do whatever He wishes with us. When we have an awesome respect for the Creator of the universe, His sayings and commandments will become increasingly important to us.

Our Lord's wisdom brings *life, health, exaltation, honor, grace, a long life, happiness, peace, riches, favor, good repute,* and more. It also brings reproof and discipline when we need it (Prov. 3:1–18).

As we reverently search our Lord's sayings and commandments, we gain His wisdom and godly counsel. Then hopefully we won't need the painful experiences that suddenly crop up when we need to "learn a lesson"!

The Power of the Tongue

As crazy as it seems, the Bible says our *speech* will determine our life or death, lack or abundance.

With the fruit of a *man's mouth* his stomach will

be satisfied; He will be satisfied with the *product of his lips. Death and life are in the power of the tongue,* and *those who love it will eat its fruit.* Proverbs 18:20–21

Words have power. Our Father delights in our knowing His word, and it never returns to Him without accomplishing what it says (Is. 55:11). He created the worlds with His word and the Holy Spirit performed it.

We are to use His word to create in our lives what we need and desire, provided His words abide in us and we abide in Him (John 15:7).

Our words impact the world around us in both the physical and the spiritual arenas. Watch carefully the words you speak. Not only do *you* hear them, but so does our Lord and the enemy. Speak *life,* which is the word of God.

The word of God is perfect and we are not to add or subtract from it in any way. Proverbs 30:5–6 says, "Every word of God is *tested* (*pure*—KJV); He is a shield to those who take refuge in Him. Do not add to His words lest He reprove you, and you be proved a liar." A single verse should not stand alone any more than one line out of a cookbook. You need to read the whole recipe when you're making a dish, don't you? The same goes for knowing the "whole counsel (Bible) of God." You need to understand the whole concept before you start trying to dissect individual sentences.

Reading the whole Bible is a big job. I know a lot of people who have started and never finished. I challenge you to ask the Father which one book from the Bible He would like you to read now. Whatever comes to mind, read it. Even if the book was your thought and not a Spirit inspired one, you will still be blessed as you drink in the word. Then ask Him to show you what He wants you to understand from your reading. You'll be surprised what He reveals to you if you will ask—*believing*.

He impressed me to read Acts six times in a row before I finally got a message He wanted me to get. It doesn't matter…it's all good!

Then when you have the word in your spirit, speak it over the circumstances in your life. You'll be amazed at what happens!

Diligence—Not Slackness—Brings Reward

Ever heard the old saying, "What goes around comes around"? One of God's spiritual laws is *we reap what we sow* (Galatians 6:7).

> I passed by the field of the sluggard, and by the vineyard of the man lacking sense; and behold, it was completely overgrown with thistles, its surface was covered with nettles, and its stone wall was broken down.
> When I saw, I reflected upon it; I looked, and received instruction. "A little sleep, a little slumber, a little folding of the hands to rest," then your poverty will come as a robber, and your want like an armed man. Proverbs 24:30–34

In these verses we see what we reap from laziness—

emptiness, ruin, and poverty. God doesn't bless laziness. He blesses hard work.

Some people want to be treated special because they are "King's kids." Unfortunately, this attitude usually helps them justify not working. They allow other people to do the work at church, home, and in the business world while they "wait on the Lord" to do it for them. This is a lazy, superior attitude that needs to be dealt with, and it begins with us.

When we work hard *because* we are "King's kids," we bring honor and glory to Him and He blesses us in all we do.

"Poor is he who works with a negligent hand, but *the hand of the diligent makes rich*" (Proverbs 10:4).

Life and Conduct

How in the world can we know what to do in every situation?

Every man's way is right in his own eyes, but the LORD weighs the hearts. *To do righteousness and justice is desired by the LORD* rather than sacrifice.

He who shuts his ear to the cry of the poor will also cry himself and not be answered. Proverbs 21:2–3, 13

Kindness, mercy, humility, justice, and righteousness are the guidelines for our conduct. All of these emanate from our Lord, and as He lives in us, they will be evident in all that we do. Checkpoint!

Moderation—Not Excess

As soldiers in the Lord's army, can we eat and drink whatever we want? Oh, we're getting to the serious stuff now! This is absolutely the hardest part for many people to incorporate into their lives.

> Do not be with *heavy* drinkers of wine, or with *gluttonous* eaters of meat; for the *heavy* drinker and the *glutton* will come to poverty, and drowsiness will clothe a man with rags. Proverbs 23:20–21

> Wine is a mocker, strong drink a brawler, and whoever is *intoxicated* by it is not wise. Proverbs 20:1

These scriptures don't say to not eat meat or drink wine. They show us the *effects of greedy appetites.*

To be gluttonous is to be greedy about food, having the habit of eating too much. Intoxication is the effect of drinking excessively. Both stem from a self-centered attitude of always wanting more and more and more and more and more.

When we see this attitude pertaining to money or power, we are quick to point it out and say, "Greedy!" But when it comes to satisfying our fleshly appetites, we look the other way saying, "Who, me?"

Eating is one of my favorite things to do. Especially desserts! My body keeps telling me, "Oh, this is delicious. Just one more bite," until I've eaten too much. When I'm struggling with it, I'll speak to my body and say, "No! You can't have any more." Then I have to remove myself from the temptation, which means out of the room!

As soldiers in our Lord's army, we need to be moderate and controlled in our behavior. Remember, many times our witness does not come from our lips, but from the example people see from our lives. Sobering, isn't it?

Justice and Victory Belong to the Lord

Have you ever wanted to take matters into your own hands and do something in retaliation when you've been wronged? Thoughts ranging from vehemently defending ourselves all the way up to bloodthirsty revenge can cross our minds when we've been treated unfairly.

Surprise! We're not supposed to do anything but turn the matter over to the Lord for His perfect justice. Then forgive them and forget about it. Sounds pretty hard, huh?!

"Do not say, 'I will repay evil'; *wait for the Lord, and He will save you*" (Proverbs 20:22).

"Many seek the ruler's favor, but *justice for man comes from the Lord*" (Proverbs 29:26).

The Lord has many ways of repaying us, *and* the guilty party for our actions. Remember, we reap what we sow.

When we first bought our home, we had three monstrous pine trees that were taller than any ancient tree in the area, in our front yard. They were close to our circular driveway, so our cars were used for target practice by a family of squirrels every time they ate their dinner of pinecones. Removing the bothersome trees soon became a priority.

I selected a local tree surgeon that assured me they were insured and would be responsible for any and all damage incurred as a result of removing the enormous trees. I started getting nervous when they began dropping large sections of the trees into the yard creating craters two to three feet deep. Then my stomach leaped into my throat when a truck piled high with pine sections dropped four feet into one of our septic tanks. The grand finale occurred when several large tree sections dropped onto the asphalt driveway, making huge cracks and dents.

I tried not to worry since the tree surgeon was supposed to be insured. But long story short, the company would not honor their initial promise of responsibility and left us with a caved in septic tank, holes in the yard, and potholes and cracks in the driveway.

Fortunately, our insurance took care of the septic tank disaster, and I was able to fill the holes in the yard. But I fumed as I continued to look at a cracked and dented driveway every time I came and went. I was furious about it for months!

Finally, I resigned the situation to the Lord and decided to forgive the tree surgeons. I was the only person getting hurt in the situation because of the bitterness I held in my heart toward a less than honest company.

I may never know what justice the Lord brought to that company, but He certainly blessed my releasing the situation to Him. Our driveway was old anyway, and a few months later when our neighborhood streets were getting repaved, a contractor for the roads repaved our entire driveway for less than half the normal cost. I was thinking a little repair, and the Lord was thinking a big new driveway!

We limit God by taking matters into our own hands. Turn over your injustices to Him and let Him be your defense. He is the best defender in the world. Trust Him. He won't let you down.

Then *forgive* and *forget* it. As long as we keep holding on to it, the Lord won't interfere. So let go and let the Lord balance the scales. In Him we will be victorious over-comers!

Endurance Leads to Eternal Life

When you train for sprints, you train hard and fast, but short distances. Marathon running requires an entirely different kind of training. You have to pace yourself and be willing to go the distance. Sometimes the Lord puts us through endurance training, so we can run life's marathons when we need to.

> ... and let us *run with endurance the race* that is set before us, fixing our eyes on Jesus, the author and perfecter of faith...Heb. 12:1b-2a

> *It is for discipline that you endure;* God deals with you as with sons; for what son is there whom his father does not discipline? Heb. 12:7

> ... *He disciplines us for our good, that we may*

share His holiness. All discipline for the moment seems not to be joyful, but sorrowful; yet to those who have been trained by it, afterwards it yields the peaceful fruit of righteousness. Heb.12:10b-11

The Lord is working on the monumental task of raising and training His children. Sometimes He allows circumstances to occur to "get our attention." Notice I said *allows* to occur, for I truly believe the Lord never sends bad things to His children. He merely removes His hedge of protection and lets us walk around in "the world." This is one way He disciplines us.

As you know, the younger the child, the more unaware of the dangers of this world. A child could play in a minefield and not know it. Without the Lord's guidance, we as spiritual children can make stupid mistakes and suffer terrible consequences. Then we have to endure.

Our heavenly Father knows how much we need Him even when we don't fully understand this yet. He patiently allows us to make mistakes and take the consequences of walking on our own. Hopefully, this enables us to see just how much we need His direction. He isn't trying to punish us but is merely allowing us the freedom to live outside His shelter if we want to.

It is our choice. We can choose to be submitted to our wonderful heavenly Father or we can follow our own desires. Just don't be surprised when you get "run over" if you are playing in the road!

Sometimes, even when we are faithfully following the Lord, we open the door to let the enemy in without realizing it. It can be through *lack of obedience* that we unlock the door. The enemy waits for the opportunity and then seizes it when we are least expecting it.

At other times the enemy can't touch us because we are right under the Lord's "wings," but he'll try to get at us through someone close who isn't under the Lord's complete protection.

Whatever the cause, when we encounter trials and tribulations, we are to endure for discipline. Jesus did it and He had a rougher road than we will ever have to travel. He knew the joy that was to come and so should we.

As we keep our eyes focused on our Lord and press through the battle of our circumstances *with Him*, our faith will be stronger when we come out on the other side. It may not be very much fun, but the perfecting of our faith will be worth it.

"And we know that *God causes all things to work together for good to those who love God,* to those who are called according to His purpose" (Romans 8:28).

Through Christ, endurance brings holiness, righteousness and eternal life. Through Him we'll finish our "race" and win the war!

Only God Counts

Got stuff? Ambitions? That's great, but we "ain't gonna" take it with us!

King Solomon wrote in Ecclesiastes 1:2, "Vanity of vanities! All is vanity."

Nothing was designed by God our Creator to last forever but the complex human spirit that lies within each one of us.

When I finally changed my perspective from the here and now to the bigger picture of life after we leave earth, I came to the realization that *only what we invest in each other will last forever.* This helped me redirect my focus onto God's plans and purposes. After all, nothing else is going to last, is it?!

> The conclusion, when all has been heard, is: *fear God and keep His commandments,* because this applies to every person. For God will bring every act to judgment, everything which is hidden, whether it is good or evil. Ecclesiastes 12:13–14

CHECKLIST

1) Have you completely *turned away from sinful behavior?*

2) Are you in the process of *humbling yourself* before the Lord?

3) What is your level of *dedication?*

4) What *instrument* are you in the Lord's orchestra? Are you "*playing*" for Him?

5) Do you have *awesome reverence* for our Creator? Are His *sayings* and *commandments* of paramount importance to you?

6) Do you speak *life* (the word) or *death?*

7) Are you a *diligent* worker? Do you seek the Lord *diligently?*

8) Are the guidelines of your conduct *kindness, mercy, humility, justice,* and *righteousness?*

9) Is your lifestyle one of *moderation?*

10) Are you allowing the Lord to be your *justice* and your *victory?*

11) Are you becoming disciplined through *endurance?*

12) Are you focused on *God's plans,* instead of yours?

When I was making the outline for this book, the name of the chapter "Hearken unto My voice" was the idea the Lord gave me. I really didn't understand what it meant in relation to the chapter, so I did a little research.

I discovered to *hearken* is to listen attentively or to pay close attention to something. The *voice* of God is His word. *If we pay very close attention to what His sayings and commandments are telling us, we will believe them and put them to use in our lives.* It is by *applying* the word that the promises become a reality to us.

The Lord gave me two illustrations of this principle. In my thoughts I heard Him say, *"How does a player hit the ball?"*

I thought to myself, *Where is this going…?* but replied, "He swings at it."

The Lord responded, *"That is like swinging at the*

scripture." Now I really didn't know what He was getting at, so I asked Him to give me another example.

He said, "*How does the bird fly?*"

I answered, "He flaps his wings?" I really didn't get what He wanted me to see.

The Lord patiently explained, "*It is not as the player swings, but as the bat meets the ball that the hit is made. It is not as the bird flaps its wings, but as the wing meets the air that the bird flies. So it is with the word of God. The scriptures without application in your life is like the swinging of the bat or the flapping of the wings. When the scripture is applied to your life, then it is like the bat meeting the ball or the bird flying in the air. Scriptures without application are meaningless. When they are applied to your life, they are victory.*"

The word of God is a creative force. By His Word, our heavenly Father created the worlds by the power of His Holy Spirit. With the word of God active in your life, you will see new beginnings, the fulfillment of hopes, and the satisfaction of work well done.

As we put into practice what the Lord reveals in His word, watch His victory come forth!

CHAPTER 8

BLESSED ASSURANCE

Part I—Unconditional Love

His Love

Have you ever wondered if God really loves you? Sometimes it seems impossible that God could love us in spite of the terrible and even the not so terrible things we do.

In my earlier years, I believed God put conditions on His love for us. There are so many lessons in the Bible about right behavior, I thought we had to be good to earn His love. This was my first mistake.

Then I learned the only way we become right with God is through Jesus. Not through our actions. I thought we had to love Jesus, repent of our sins, and stay faithful to Him to receive His love. My second mistake.

One late, summer evening when I was taking a walk, I shared with the Lord my frustration in not being able to maintain a holy lifestyle. All of a sudden, I felt peace and acceptance envelop me like comforting arms wrapping around me in a warm embrace. At that instant I understood He doesn't expect us to get everything right. He looks at the intentions of our heart and our desire to please Him much more than our successes. Like most loving parents, He expects us to try our best, but even that isn't a condition for His love.

God's love is unconditional. *Unconditional love is an absolute love. A love with no conditions!* We don't have to be good, righteous, or even very nice for God to love us. He loves us because it is His nature (1 John 4:8).

The way He loves us reminds me of my love for a dog I had for thirteen years. Cissy was a very smart, wiry-haired gray mutt that I rescued from the dog pound. People always said how ugly she was, but I thought she was completely adorable. I loved Cissy no matter what she looked like or what she did. When Cissy was good I rewarded her, and when she was bad I disciplined her. I loved her no less when she chewed up my shoes and dug holes in the yard. It made me furious, but I still loved her! She was quite an escape artist, and when she went on her excursions I would spend hours anxiously driving up and down neighborhood streets calling her name, looking until I found her. But I was tolerant of her misdeeds because I knew she was a dog and had the nature of a dog.

I believe God loves us no matter what we do. That doesn't mean He approves of us doing wrong things, but He never quits loving us.

It is comforting to know that we don't have to earn His love in any way. All we need to do is love Him in return.

Just as my dog wanted to please me out of her devotion, we will try to obey our Master's commandments and follow His instruction because of our love for Him—but it's not a contingency for His love.

I can't begin to imagine the tremendous love of our Father, who was willing to let His perfect Son die an excruciating death for the benefit of His other children. Furthermore, I can barely comprehend the love of Jesus, who willingly and with full awareness endured that horrendous, torturous death for our sake. We must never forget it!

> For He was foreknown before the foundation of the world, *but has appeared in these last times for the sake of you* who through Him are believers in God, who raised Him from the dead and gave Him glory, so that your faith and hope are in God.
> 1 Peter 1:20–21

Our Love

Our Lord wants us to love others with the same unconditional love He gives to us. Even the strange ones! I remind myself sometimes when I meet someone who seems odd, that they are just as lovable to the Lord as wire-haired, ugly old Cissy was to me.

"Since you have in obedience to the truth purified your souls for a sincere love of the brethren, *fervently love one another from the heart*" (1 Peter 1:22).

Do you have a hard time loving people who don't act

nice? I do! Some people are just hard to be around. I want everyone to be happy and enthusiastic, and when I'm with people that are negative or abrasive, I don't like it. I have to make a conscious decision to let Jesus love them *through* me, because I can't love them without His help. But it can be done through Him.

You know what it's like to have someone hurt your feelings. It's hard to forgive them, much less love them. One Palm Sunday when I was still very new at St. Peter's church, I arrived to see people wandering around outside with palmetto branches, instead of going into the church building. I didn't know what to do and said anxiously out loud, "What in the world are we supposed to be doing?" A lady walking by heard me and turned around and quickly snapped, "If you were here earlier you would know what to do!" I had to blink back the tears and breathe deeply so no one would see how her words had affected me. It felt as if she had slapped my face!

I avoided her at all costs for years, until the fated day I began a new class at church. Guess who showed up the first night of this class? You got it. The lady I was trying to avoid. I know God has a sense of humor, but I didn't think that was very funny.

The week prior to taking the class, every time I turned on the radio I was bombarded with teachings on forgiveness. After seeing who was in my class, I began to get the picture. It wasn't very hard to figure out that God wanted me to forgive her.

I certainly didn't feel very forgiving, but I knew what I needed to do. I told Jesus I would choose to forgive her, but

I didn't have any of my own forgiveness to give. I needed Him to let His love flow through me—to her. After a few weeks, I realized I no longer had any animosity towards her. Surprisingly, this lady and I became good friends through the course of the class and remained close for many years. Once I was willing, the Lord could do His work in me and through me.

> Beloved, *let us love one another, for love is from God;* and everyone who loves is born of God and knows God. The one who does not love does not know God, *for God is love.*
>
> By this *the love of God was manifested in us,* that God has sent His only begotten Son into the world *so that we might live through Him.* In this is love, not that we loved God, but that He loved us and sent His Son to be the propitiation for our sins.
>
> Beloved, *if God so loved us, we also ought to love one another.* 1 John 4:7–11

As God fills us, His supernatural love overflows out of us to others. Whether they are good or bad, loving or not, we simply make a decision to get out of our natural reaction and let God's love flow through us. Only through Him can we really love others.

We, as the body of Christ, should especially try to get along with one another. When we fuss, fight, or avoid one another, we're like a hand that's at war with itself. How ridiculous would it be if the thumb was fighting the fourth finger and the pinky was trying to avoid the second finger? The hand wouldn't be able to do much, would it?

Neither can the body of Christ, when it's fighting among itself or avoiding offending members.

If we're not going to be a handicapped body of believers, let's be reconciled and allow the love of the Lord to flow through us. Then as we work in unison, we'll be able to stand against the enemy and minister to those in need.

Part II—"Seek My Face"

My cousin Theresa asks the Lord for help with everything. She "seeks His face" about traffic conditions, the best stores to shop for particular items, when to go places and what to do when she gets there. You know what? I've seen the Lord come through for her over and over again. She avoids traffic accidents, finds great buys, and arrives at places "coincidentally" at the same time someone else does she needs to talk to. Most importantly, when she seeks the Lord, she trusts He will answer her.

The Lord wants to help us with the big and little things in our lives, but He usually won't interfere if we don't ask for His help. He responds to our trust and faith in Him, as we expectantly reach out to Him and wait for His presence and response. This is called "seeking His face." When we look to Him, He shows up in special ways to help us. If we don't look to Him, He usually will not interfere in our lives.

The following group of scriptures shows different circumstances in believer's lives brought before God for

His guidance and intervention. Look at the marvelous things that can happen when we seek the Lord:

1. *Supernatural Power*

These *all with one mind were continually devoting themselves to prayer,* along with the women, and Mary the mother of Jesus, and with His brothers.

And when the day of Pentecost had come, they were all together in one place. And *suddenly there came from heaven a noise like a violent, rushing wind, and it filled the whole house* where they were sitting. And *there appeared to him tongues as of fire distributing themselves, and they rested on each one of them. And they were all filled with the Holy Spirit and began to speak with other tongues,* as the Spirit was giving them utterance. Acts 1:14, 2:1–4

Several years ago, I was diagnosed with degenerating ligaments in my shoulders. When I rotated my arms, it sounded like the ligaments in my shoulders were snapping and popping like rubber bands. My shoulders ached all of the time, and the pain drained my energy. My doctor informed me that kind of ligament problem would never get better, only worse.

One Sunday my shoulders were unbearable, so I approached the waiting prayer team at the back of the church. They prayed for me and the power of God came upon me so strongly, that my legs felt like Jell-O. I tried to stand, but was so wobbly, they gently laid me on the floor with understanding patience. They continued to pray for me, and I couldn't help but think how funny I must look lying on the floor. I giggled and giggled and felt so peaceful and happy.

Even though I was still feeling pretty peaceful, I knew I couldn't lie there on the floor all day, so after a little while I decided I better get up. I was amazed when I reached back and pushed myself up. There was no pain! My arms and shoulders were healed from that moment forward. What supernatural power!

2. *Divine Appointment*

> And *they prayed,* and said, "Thou, LORD, who knowest the hearts of all men, show which one of these two Thou hast chosen to occupy this ministry and apostleship from which Judas turned aside to go to his own place." And *they drew lots for them, and the lot fell to Matthias; and he was numbered with the eleven apostles.* Acts 1:24–26

This scripture refers to a divine selection. However, I'd like to share with you another type of divine appointment. A little prayer group I met with at work was trying to meet during the lunch hour. We were disappointed as first one person had to leave early and then another.

With only two of us remaining, we began to pray. All of a sudden, I saw the words "wounded spirit." I asked the woman who was praying with me if she was the wounded spirit, and she said, "Yes." As we continued to pray, I saw a picture of her holding onto a black book, which was the past.

After we prayed cleansing prayers for her, we both acknowledged that it was interesting how God arranged for just the two of us to be there for a special time of ministering. We both had an overwhelming sense we were placed together at that moment, for a divine appointment, or in other words a special prearranged meeting orchestrated by God.

I am still awed when I think how much He loves this woman to have arranged the details of the meeting for her benefit. And He loves each of us like that!

3. *Holy Boldness*

And when they heard this, *they lifted their voices to God with one accord* and said, "O LORD, it is Thou who didst make the heaven and the earth and the sea, and all that is in them..." *And when they had prayed, the place where they had gathered together was shaken, and they were all filled with the Holy Spirit, and began to speak the word of God with boldness.* Acts 4:24, 31

I used to be afraid that I would be ridiculed if I let others know about my experiences with the Lord. I have seen such incredible things that I knew it would be hard for people to believe, much less accept. So I didn't tell very many people.

The Lord kept dealing with me to not be ashamed of what I have seen Him do...so I began to pray for holy boldness. I didn't have any earth shaking experience, but gradually found I was getting bolder about sharing Jesus when the opportunity arose. Which has been huge for me!

4. *Raising the Dead*

[A godly woman named Tabitha fell sick and died. Her friends went for Peter and brought him back to the room where her body was…] But *Peter sent them all out and knelt down and prayed,* and turning to the body, he said, "Tabitha, arise." *And she opened her eyes, and when she saw Peter, she sat up.* Acts 9:36–40

I have heard some wonderful, incredible stories of people being raised from the dead, but the story I want to share with you involves a pet fish! My cousin Theresa and her son had a nice, big aquarium with large, very well fed fish in it. One day, Theresa's son Patrick noticed one of the fish was floating belly up with bulging white eyes. He tearfully asked his mother if his fish was dead, to which she quickly responded, "Let's ask God to bring him back to life!"

She then realized what she had said and quickly uttered a silent prayer, "God, you've got to do this one for Patrick!" Then she and Patrick asked the Lord to bring their fish back to life…well, you know the rest of the story. The fish flipped over and swam away! Maybe it was only a fish, but it made a profound statement to a little boy. And his mother!

5. *Visions*

> ...a devout man, and one who feared God
> with all his household, and gave many alms to the
> Jewish people, *and prayed to God continually.* About
> the ninth hour of the day *he clearly saw in a vision
> an angel of God* who had just come in to him, and
> said to him, "Cornelius!" Acts 10:2–3

The kind of vision Cornelius had was an open-eyed vision. He apparently saw the angel with his eyes. But let's talk about the more common closed-eyed visions seen on the canvas of the mind.

When I get a "picture" when I'm praying, it will normally stay frozen in place until I ask for the meaning of it. One time I decided to see what the intercessors in our church did, so I visited their group one morning. While we were praying quietly for the list of prayer requests that had been given to them, I saw a large pair of hands with palms and fingers touching like praying hands. I could also see a doll clasped in between the praying hands. The picture didn't go away during a lengthy time of prayer, so I asked if it was a picture from Him and if it was, what it meant. The words dropped into my spirit, *"You are playing at praying."* I was stunned! I perceived this was a word for all of us, but I didn't want to tell these nice ladies who took several hours a week to pray for others this message!

I put it off and tried to dismiss it from my mind, but the picture wouldn't go away, so I timidly tried to share the picture. As you can imagine, it didn't go over very well, but as we sought the Lord further, He remonstrated, "Where is the weeping and fasting between the porch and the pillar for my people?" His message was to get more serious about praying for His people.

The Lord will give us visions when it suits His purpose. Be open, but question and test them. Then take a step out in faith. If you don't, you probably will never know the Lord's purpose for the vision.

6. *Voice of God*

> And on the next day, as they were on their way, and approaching the city, Peter went up on the housetop about the sixth hour *to pray….And again a voice came to him* a second time, "What God has cleansed, no longer consider unholy." Acts 10:9, 15

The voice of God can be as loud as thunder or as soft as a whisper. In my experience, His voice comes either during prayer or after worship. When I received instruction to write this book, I had been praying and worshiping the Lord for nearly an hour. I wasn't expecting to hear anything at the time, I was just seeking His face. And then He spoke to my spirit…you know the rest.

7. *Angels*

> So Peter was kept in the prison, *but prayer for him was being made fervently by the church to God….* And behold, *an angel of the LORD suddenly appeared,* and a light shone in the cell; and he struck Peter's

side and roused him, saying, "Get up quickly." And his chains fell off his hands. Acts 12:5, 7

I am sure we are touched by angels all the time and aren't aware of it. A few years ago a fellow that worked for my parents relayed an incident that his pastor had that week. The pastor was driving between two little towns outside of Gainesville, Florida, when he saw a nice-looking clean-cut young man beside the road. He stopped and picked the young man up intending to share the love of Jesus with him.

As they drove, he told the young man of his denomination's ten-year plan to evangelize the world. The young man turned to him and said, "What makes you think you have ten years?" and immediately disappeared!

The pastor nearly had heart failure over his vanishing rider. Was it an angel? I don't know, but it certainly made for interesting discussion!

8. *Holy Spirit's Guidance*

And *while they were ministering to the* LORD *and fasting, the Holy Spirit said,* "Set apart for Me Barnabas and Saul for the work to which I have called them." Then, *when they had fasted and prayed* and laid their hands on them, they sent them away. Acts 13:2–3

A few years ago, I pulled the vertebrae in my back out of alignment. I prayed and was impressed, "*A physician is necessary.*" So away I went to a doctor of osteopath, who adjusted my back into place the first visit. Blessed relief!

A week later it slipped back out, and I prayed for guidance and got, "*A physician is not necessary.*" I didn't like that answer. After all, He advised me to go to a doctor the last time, didn't He? In frustration I decided to call for an appointment with the same doctor because I was in excruciating pain. The only problem was, it was Friday afternoon at 4:00. Guess what? No appointments were available.

That night I drove to my parent's house an hour and a half away, in tearful agony. Leaving my young children in the car and without saying hello to my parents, I crept straight toward their bathtub and possible relief.

As I lay in the steaming tub not knowing how I was going to endure the pain any longer, I started to turn over on my side to keep warm. All of a sudden my hip slipped on the smooth enamel surface of the bathtub and my knee dropped over the other knee quickly. *Crack, crack, crack, crack,* went all the vertebrae in my lower back. To my surprise my back was feeling better! I gingerly turned over on the other side and repeated the same action and again I heard *crack, crack, crack, crack.* Ahhh…much better. It was sore but back in place. I sheepishly apologized to the Lord for doubting His guidance. Sometimes we have to learn the hard way.

9. *Healing*

> And it came about that the father of Publius was lying in bed afflicted with recurrent fever and dysentery; and Paul went in to see him *and after he had prayed, he laid his hands on him and healed him.*
> Acts 28:8

My daughter Heather is my best example of healing by prayer. She always believed the Lord would heal her when we sought Him and prayed…and He did. It didn't really sink in how much we had relied on the Lord for her healing over the years until she had to get a physical before summer camp when she was fifteen. The doctor looked in amazement at her chart and commented that she hadn't been in for a visit since she was a little girl.

I told him when she was sick we just prayed for her and she got well. With an incredulous look, he shook his head and gave her a check-up!

In the preceding sections, the scriptures reveal what happens when we seek the Lord's face. *Supernatural results occur after seeking the Lord through prayer.* Supernatural results happened because of the prayer of faith that went up *first.*

Neither Peter nor Paul laid hands on the dead or sick without praying *first. After* they prayed, the Holy Spirit ministered through them.

The body of believers prayed *first,* and then the Holy Spirit filled them and they spoke with tongues.

They prayed *first,* and Peter was miraculously released from prison by an angel.

After the church at Antioch ministered to the Lord and fasted, the Holy Spirit gave them instruction for sending out Barnabas and Saul.

After Cornelius' continuous prayers and Peter's daily prayers, they were given separate visions with a message from the Lord. All of these prayers were offered up in faith, trusting that God would reveal Himself to them as He saw fit.

Many if not most times, people rush into solving their problems with a quick prayer on the way, if they remember to pray at all. As we seek God about our problems, and trust He will help us with them, He responds.

Some people think they will only "bother God" if there is an important decision to be made or a big need. But He is never too busy for us, and no problem or circumstance is too trivial for Him. When we think of Him first, the Holy Spirit has a much better chance of getting our Father's ideas across to us. We might even be receptive and do them!

Our Lord is a God of the natural and the supernatural. When you seek Him and His desires in all things, He'll move in exciting ways in your life!

Part III—Prepare

Accept Jesus Unconditionally

How many times have you heard the term "accepting Jesus"? When I hear that term, I normally think of people receiving Jesus as their personal Savior. But there is more involved to really accept Him.

To accept Him is to *take or receive what is offered or given by Him*…to *say yes* to Him…to *believe* Him…to *receive* Him *with liking* and approval…to *undertake* His priorities *as a responsibility*…to *receive* Him and what He brings *as satisfactory.* To accept Him is to *understand* Him.[16]

Puts a different slant on things, doesn't it? Jesus freely offers Himself and His authority to His followers. It's up to us to *take and receive what He offers.* He may stand there with packages of healing in His arms, but it's up to us to reach out and receive it.

One time when I was worshiping the Lord, I saw a picture in my mind of a big room full of beautiful presents. They were richly decorated and even seemed to glow. I asked the Lord what the picture meant, and He showed me they were unclaimed gifts. He wanted to give them to His children, but they didn't know they were there and consequently didn't reach out and take them. Then I could see in the beautiful boxes. There were legs and eyes and clothes and toys and all sorts of things. The room was so rich and lovely, but the very air was permeated with the sadness of a loving Father who ached to give His children the things they were longing for. I thought, *If only they knew their gifts were just waiting for them to receive!*

He also may want to give us something we don't want. Like the life of a servant. Can we accept that also? Come on. We can do all things through Christ who strengthens us!

Can we *say yes* to Him without any conditions?

Accepting the lordship of Jesus in my life, changed who made the decisions. Instead of asking myself, "What do I want to do?" I substitute, "Lord, what do You want me to do?" I now *say yes* to His plans instead of my own. And you know what? His plans always work out for the best.

To accept Jesus is to *believe* Him, no matter what the world or circumstances say differently. Believing the words He spoke are truth and anything contradictory is the opposite of truth—a lie.

Jesus was the Word, He is the Word and always will be the Word. Even though He was not made flesh until the time of the New Testament, He was alive and speaking by the power of the Holy Spirit through the prophets in the Old Testament. He is still speaking to us today. We must *believe* the Word (who is Jesus), unconditionally.

Do you *like and approve* of Jesus or do you *use* Him in times of need? A good friendship is based on mutual respect, admiration, and caring. A bad friendship occurs when only one of the parties gives and cares.

I had a friend growing up who was a lot of fun, but she wasn't really interested in how I felt about things or when I had hurts or needs. She primarily wanted someone to listen to her and be interested in her life. I became weary of a lop-sided relationship and eventually spent little time with her.

Ask yourself the question, "Do I have a mutual loving relationship with Jesus or do I always stand on the receiving end?" To accept Jesus is to have a mutual caring friendship.

When we accept Jesus Christ as Lord and Savior, we

have a *responsibility* to follow Him as a disciple. That means learning His principles and putting them into place in our lives. Most of us are childish enough at heart to want to have the benefits from the relationship without the rigors of discipline that come with following Christ. When we truly accept Him, we also accept the *responsibility* of following in His footsteps.

The life we pursue as a soldier in His army is a victorious one. But there is sacrifice, hard work, and dedication involved. He wants us to be *satisfied* with what He offers. It took me a long time to realize that when I wasn't satisfied with what I had, in effect I was saying to Him I wasn't satisfied with what He was offering me. When I changed my attitude, I became more content and appreciative of my surroundings and circumstances.

If we accept Jesus, we will try to *understand Him.* Jesus is so simple and yet so complex. His life of loving kindness, mercy, and vulnerability are so easy to see, and yet He is so profound, we will spend our lifetime coming into a full knowledge of Him. To accept Jesus is to enjoy a lifetime of new revelation and understanding concerning who He is to us.

Accepting Jesus unconditionally means receiving Him and going through life's journey on His track. With no contingencies. A bit challenging, but from Jesus' perspective, the alternatives don't work.

> And another also said, "I will follow You, Lord; but first permit me to say goodbye to those at home." But Jesus said to him, "No one, after

putting his hand to the plow and looking back, is fit for the kingdom of God." Luke 9:61–62

Jesus gave His *all*. Will you give Him yours?

"Get Ready for My Return"

There are many people predicting the Lord will return very soon. One day when my daughter Kaitlin was twenty-one months old, we were enjoying some praise music together. Without any prompting she looked up with bright eyes and exclaimed, "Jesus is coming!"

The Bible says the Lord is coming back for His bride (the church) to take us away with Him. We don't know if He is coming back a long time from now, or much sooner. But what if He comes for *you* tonight? "*Be on the alert then, for you do not know the day nor the hour*" (Matthew 25:13).

Are you ready? Ask yourself:

1) *Have I washed my "robes" or actions in His spiritual blood?* Am I living a pure and holy lifestyle, where my behavior is right? When I slip and sin, do I immediately repent and return to the Lord's side?

2) *Is my family ready?* Have I invested in my children the ways of the Lord? Have I prepared for their future?

3) *Have I completed my assignments?* If the Lord put in your spirit a desire to preach, have you done it? If He impressed you to speak of Him to someone you know, did you respond? If He told you to do a work for Him, were you obedient? Can you stand before

Him and say, "Job complete, sir!" If not, are you ready for His return?

The Lord wants us to come to Him with *no regrets. Owing no man!* And *prepared.* In the story of the ten virgins told in Matthew 25, only half of them were prepared for their bridegroom. When the bridegroom unexpectedly came back, some were ready for him. Some were not.

[Jesus said,] *"For this reason you be ready too; for the Son of Man is coming at an hour when you do not think He will. Who then is the faithful and sensible slave whom his master put in charge of his household to give them their food at the proper time? Blessed is that slave whom his master finds so doing when he comes. Truly I say to you, that he will put him in charge of all his possessions.*

"But if that evil slave says in his heart, 'My master is not coming for a long time,' and shall begin to beat his fellow slaves and eat and drink with drunkards; the master of that slave will come on a day when he does not expect him and at an hour which he does not know, and shall cut him in pieces and assign him a place with the hypocrites; weeping shall be there and the gnashing of teeth."
Matthew 24:44–51

Let us prepare and draw close to the Lord, so when He returns for us, we can rush into His waiting arms with no regrets!

CHECKLIST

1) Do you *choose* to *love others* through the power of God's love?

2) Are you *seeking the Lord's face* in *all* things? Are you praying in faith, trusting in His response?

3) Do you *accept Jesus unconditionally?* Are you giving Him your all?

4) Are you *prepared* and *ready* for our Lord's return? With no regrets?

We all need "*blessed assurance*" to see us through the days ahead. Assurance that Jesus is here for us with guidelines, instruction, and approval.

We receive this blessed assurance through His word and the fulfillment of it in our lives. It is the answer of those who seek His face. Blessed assurance is *Jesus fulfilling the scripture.* It is available for all in our Lord's kingdom.

The guidelines for kingdom living are tough if not impossible to enact without an ongoing, intimate relationship with our Commander-in-Chief. But with that wondrous relationship comes the most incredible power, peace, provision, joy, and love. I know you will find indescribable fulfillment as you travel on your journey with Him.

I look forward to one day hearing what wonderful times *you* have had with the Lord!

ENDNOTES

1. James Strong, LL.D., S.T.D., *The New Strong's Exhaustive Concordance of the Bible* (Nashville: Thomas Nelson Publishers, 1984) p. 70 Greek Dictionary

2. *World Book Dictionary* (A Thorndike-Barnhart Dictionary, 1987) p. 1156

3. James Strong, LL.D., S.T.D., *The New Strong's Exhaustive Concordance of the Bible* (Nashville: Thomas Nelson Publishers, 1984) p. 38 Hebrew and Chaldee Dictionary

4. Ibid, p. 10 Greek Dictionary

5. James Strong, LL.D., S.T.D., *The New Strongs Exhaustive Concordance of the Bible* (Nashville: Thomas Nelson Publishers, 1984) p.74 Greek Dictionary

6. James Strong, LL.D., S.T.D., *The New Strongs Exhaustive Concordance of the Bible* (Nashville:

Thomas Nelson Publishers, 1984) p.57 Hebrew Dictionary

7. *World Book Dictionary* (A Thorndike-Barnhart Dictionary, 1987) p. 1156

8. Ibid., p. 2156

9. Ibid., p. 1625

10. *World Book Dictionary* (A Thorndike-Barnhart Dictionary, 1987) p. 2047

11. James Strong, LL.D., S.T.D., *The New Strongs Exhaustive Concordance of the Bible* (Nashville: Thomas Nelson Publishers, 1984) p. 102 Hebrew Dictionary

12. Merrill F. Unger, *The New Unger's Bible Dictionary* (Chicago: Moody Press, 1988) p. 1040–1041

13. Porter Barrington, "The Christian Life Study Outlines and Notes," *The Open Bible* (Thomas Nelson Publishers, 1979) Sec. V, p. 1127

14. *World Book Dictionary* (A Thorndike-Barnhart Dictionary, 1987) p. 417

15. Ibid., p. 542

16. *World Book Dictionary* (A Thorndike-Barnhart Dictionary, 1987) p. 12